Inspired by Method

creative tools for the design process

Contents

Key

→   go to page

G   check glossary

↓   keywords

Inspired by Method

What is inspiration?
Can there be a method for achieving it?

Inspiration is an essential part of any successful creative process. But as I have noticed in my many years of teaching at design and art schools as well as in design offices, there is often no coherent approach in place. Over the years, I have developed a method of creativity that enables people to make the most of their potential. The method can be categorised as innovation research and is based both on traditional teaching methods and on current specialist knowledge. It should be the golden thread guiding you through the creative process. Do not see it as a straitjacket, but as an aid to help you find your way. Based on its process-oriented structure and the five transferable dimensions, the method can also be adapted to future developments in the hybrid discipline of design. You can, in principle, use these five dimensions in any design project.

This book is both a guide to and a source of inspiration. Our design approach relies on a mix of individuality and a clear methodology, and these are applied – whether consciously or subconsciously – in accordance with the particular project. The 5D method for inspiration described in Part A is an incisive little tool that you can use in any design process, including those you are starting from scratch.

The first phase will loosen up your thinking and set you on your way. The second phase allows you to experiment and explore some unusual paths. The third phase will reward you with your finished project.

Who is this book for? For all budding creatives involved in design in the broadest sense who want to deepen their knowledge and intellectual portfolio professionally and develop their creative skills further. The book does not require special skills, such as programming knowledge. You can "work through" this book in a completely analogue fashion. Activate your senses and imagination, learn from analyses and experiments, and get a feel for non-linear ways of working.

You can train your ability to act, think and reflect in a coherent, interconnected way, accepting the idea that linear is not always best. In the future, creativity, process competence, and flexible thinking will be an essential professional skill. A Delphi study has also made this clear.[1] In an age of artificial intelligence[G] and algorithm-based technologies, human capacities, such as creativity and (design) competence, that allow us to confidently handle agile processes are becoming increasingly important.

My method is based on transformation[G]. Knowledge, context, and material, cultural, and formal elements are transformed into something new. A plea for the sensual, the unpredictable, the unconventional, the surprising.

In **Part A** of the book I present the method. Each chapter description is visually accompanied by one example of a realised study project. Words with a superscript [G] are explained in the glossary.

In **Part B,** you will be accompanied by sessions tailored to each section. They serve to sharpen your perception[G], completely independent of your concrete project. If you work in a team, I recommend these pages from page 96.

Part C illustrates ideas for immediate implementation. These ideas all derive from exercises, studies, and projects that use the 5D method and which I have supervised. They should be stimulating and inspire you to get started yourself.

In this book, I would like to bridge the gap between a world undergoing radical change and the small, subtle role designers play in it. As Gillian Crampton Smith says: "We don't merely have to ask if we are designing the things right, we have to ask if we are designing the right things."[2] Don't shy away from socially relevant topics. Good design is an attitude – and design is an intellectual and emotional process that combines many different elements. Find your place in it, determine what you are working on and with whom.

The method presented here offers you an introduction to the creative process in the form of creative-scientific inspiration. It will give wings to your imagination, allowing you to recognise inspiration when it comes and use it for yourself. Be inspired by your project and have the courage to try things out. Wild ideas can always be tamed. Humour is allowed.

This book will give you a tool enabling you to approach your projects in a more multifaceted way and your ideas will always be ahead of the pack. There's one gift I'd like to give you along the way: you're allowed to fail – it brings new insights. Don't lose your sense of humour, just carry on. Reading this book will encourage and reward your curiosity and open-mindedness. I hope you enjoy lateral thinking and the mental kick that comes with it – it's the elixir of creativity.

Alexandra Martini

Inspiration springs from the pleasure of perception, from the fertile soil of thinking, and from the composure that allows you to deal with what comes.

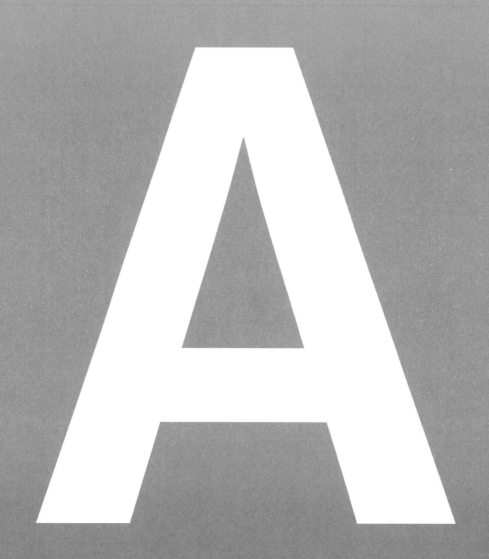

The three phases of the 5D method are described in part A. Each phase is exemplified by a single student project that accompanies you visually through the nine steps. Have fun exploring the potential of analysing, experimenting, and realising with the five dimensions!

The Process at a Glance

I provide you with a toolkit that you can always fall back on in the future. Start by abandoning any preconceptions you have about the outcome. The method^G structures the design process^G but does not lead directly to the perfect design solution – instead, it encourages you to connect familiar elements in a new way. You get off the beaten track, because going round the houses is a sure way to improve your knowledge of the local terrain. You learn to ask yourself the right questions at the right time. The following elementary aspects of design, the five dimensions of reality, will help you. They give the 5D method its name:

1. What does it look like?
   Formal-Aesthetic Dimension
2. What is it made of?
   Material-Haptic Dimension
3. How is it made?
   Productive Dimension
4. In what cultural context does it operate?
   Cultural Dimension
5. What relationships does it create?
   Interactive Dimension

These dimensions will be useful to you in each of the method's three phases:

The **first phase** is about analysing^G. You will learn how to observe the world using the five dimensions and the art of visualising^G.

In the **second phase** you will explore the five dimensions experimentally^G. You will enter the "laboratory^G", which can be any place you decide to work.

The **third phase** involves realising, completing, and documenting the project.

As a starting point for exploring inspiration in the design process, I take an example of one artistic work in the description of the 5D method. In it, these five dimensions are finely calibrated to one another.

The first time you read the book, I recommend that you go through the steps in order. Researching[G] and documenting will keep cropping up. Once you have internalised the process and the dimensions, you can always come back to individual steps or skip some. You can go through the method in a few hours or several days. With a little practice, quickly observing your environment in a few seconds will lead to inspiration.

Here's a brief overview of the mental processes involved:

When you analyse, you work inductively[G], primarily training transformative thinking, the mental linking of language, words, writing, images, and spatial imagination, where you associate[G], create analogies, find metaphors, visualise[G], and abstract.

When you experiment[G], you act abductively[G] and alternate divergent and convergent thinking by combining[G] ideas and finding out and deducing constraints and variables in order to take the next step.

When you realise, in a process of synthesis[G], you deductively[G] train the convergent thinking that your mind has access to for logical reasoning[G] and decision making as it fine-tunes your ideas.

Art and literature should help us to get out of our mental cocoons.
—ELIF SAFAK

5D Method

1
Selecting, Contextualising, and Researching
Clarifying the context of your own project
Sensitising

2
Describing, Sorting, and Evaluating
Intensifying
One work in focus
The five dimensions

5
Combining and Trying Out
Experimenting in the five dimensions
Scope, keywords, dimensions

5.1
Experimenting in the
Formal-Aesthetic Dimension

5.2
Experimenting in the
Material-Haptic Dimension

5.3
Experimenting in the
Productive Dimension

7
Completing
Executing
Implementing all dimensions

8
Presenting
Planning, packaging, selling

Analysing

The first phase serves as a source of inspiration for the project you have planned. You analyse a creative strategy[G], working approach, and mode of implementation. You collect soft and hard facts. The keywords you work with in phases two and three will get charged by your imagination.

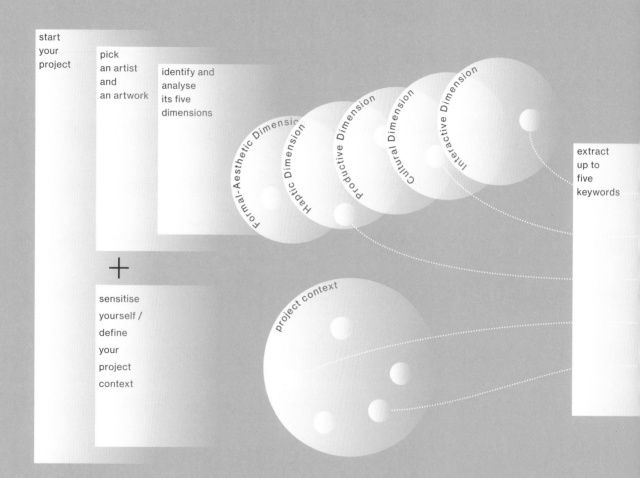

start
your
project

pick
an artist
and
an artwork

identify and
analyse
its five
dimensions

Formal-Aesthetic Dimension

Haptic Dimension

Productive Dimension

Cultural Dimension

Interactive Dimension

extract
up to
five
keywords

+

sensitise
yourself /
define
your
project
context

project context

1   **Selecting,
    Contextualising, Researching**
    Find a creative person, do
    some research, and clarify
    the scope of the project.

2   **Describing, Sorting, and Evaluating**
    Systematically record (in words) the five
    dimensions of a work of art. Choose
    the keywords that inspire you.

"The method introduced me to new approaches in design analysis and experimental design. They still support me in my daily work as a UX designer. Ultimately, it has little to do with the artist, but he or she is the primary anchor for my work, supplying me with creative ideas, keywords, and new conceptual approaches ... i.e. thinking and acting from other perspectives or out of the box."

EDMUNDO GALLINDO, INTERACTION DESIGNER

"I have learned that a systematic approach to experimentation is incredibly helpful! Even in later design projects it has been beneficial to conduct a structured analysis and create visual variants in order to develop surprising concepts."

PAULA SCHUSTER, DESIGN RESEARCHER

"Analysing with this method helps me come up with gold-plated ideas – for example, if I want to develop creative concepts out of nothing."

PHILIPP EMDE, COMMUNICATION DESIGNER

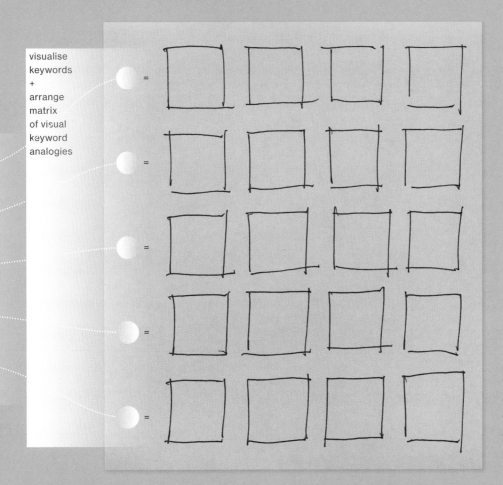

visualise
keywords
+
arrange
matrix
of visual
keyword
analogies

Note:
Visualisations
will influence
your future
decisions
positively

3 **Visualising**
Use different representational
methods to visualise the keywords.
Arrange your images in a collage.

4 **Grasping** (optional)
To help understand the process,
interpret some of the details
of the selected work.

1
Selecting, Contextualising, and Researching

Clarifying the context of your own project
Sensitising

Choose the work of a creative figure and describe what you see. Roughly define the scope/parameters of the project.

Artist:
Ai WeiWei

Scope of the project:
**casting technique
object/installation**

Example project by
Julia Bohle, Tabea Rocke, Lydia Wilke

Forever Bicycles, Ai Wei Wei, 2012

Idea

We can gather inspiration from different directions. On the one hand, we can transfer creative processes and channel the potential of other artists; on the other, we can reflect more acutely on the scope – that is the options, parameters[G], and context[G] – of our own project. Imagine the creative person – be it a designer, architect, artist, fashion designer, or motion graphic specialist – is sitting next to you in the train. During the journey, you start talking and have a stimulating conversation about the exciting things the person has done in the past. At the end she or he gives you an important take-home message.

However, creativity is always context dependent. The context of our actions, our design, and our projects is so critical that we need to open up a space that is rich in potential within which we want to carry out our project. By scope, we mean the real requirements, wishes, intentions, specifications, and conditions governing a project. The parameters for this may be given or self-defined.

Challenge

First, get an overview of the work and working methods of a creative person. Don't just consult the Internet – use a public library with a wide selection of resources. The person you choose will support you through the first phase of the method, after which you will bid her or him farewell. Don't spend too much time dithering! Just pick out someone whose name you wrote down during your last visit to the museum, for example. Inspiration lurks everywhere. Explore and research! Research always doubles up as inspiration. Researching will show up in every phase in very different forms. Then answer the following questions: When and where did the creative person live? What was the focus of their work? How did they make a name for themselves and what else do they do? What media did they work with? What working methods do they use? What else do you need to know about them?

Next, research the context in which your project will take place. Position yourself in this context and sensitise yourself to a topic. You can also adjust your own specifications in the course of the project. Clarify how much time you have. In addition, define the general context (your cultural milieu, for example) in which the project is to emerge. Normally, we understand and probe the content of any topic we are about to work on. At this point, it is not about knowing all the variables but about having a rough understanding of the options and possibilities. If the context of your project (scope) is completely new to you, then explore in greater detail those aspects of it that seem relevant to you. For example, you might wish to do a free project and have special ideas for a material, or you might have a concrete work assignment that you orientate yourself to. Select the basic ingredients now! If you want to work with light, research where you can encounter the phenomenon of light; if you have a moulding technique in mind, find out how it operates; if you want to design a poster, note the basic poster sizes.

But don't limit your openness to what the project may become. Finish by noting down the most important points and then put them aside so that you can continue analysing[G] the artistic work in the next chapter.

Objective

You will experience positive interference as your own ideas evolve when you research two topics at the same time. You will understand a specific creative way of working and the effects that the overall conditions (context/parameters) can have on projects.

   Note: The purpose of the first phase of the method is to train your perception and your capacity for abstraction. Anything from your surroundings can be suitable for this. You determine what receives your attention. The book focuses on art as a source of inspiration, but fashion, technology, and everyday culture are also suitable. If you systematically study a simple everyday object with your trained eye after you have run the method for the first time, can this be the thing that inspires you – to create, say, a visual[G]?

Creativity is always context dependent.

Inspiration lurks everywhere.

2

Describing, Sorting, and Evaluating

Intensifying
One work in focus
The five dimensions

Here you apply the five dimensions analytically for the first time by defining a small number of keywords for your own project.

1. What does it look like?
Formal-Aesthetic Dimension

varies each time in
composition and
number of bicycles
geometric
iterative
silvery
shiny
technical
loud

2. What is it made of?
Material-Haptic Dimension

bicycle frames
readymade
metal
stainless steel
repetitive

3. How is it made?
Productive Dimension

built structure
architectural form
offset

4. In what cultural context does it operate?
Cultural Dimension

human rights
freedom of expression
China
political
critical
traditional
finding a voice with art
twisted
international
luxury/status symbol
symbolic
environmental

5. What relationships does it create?
Interactive Dimension

hypnotic
spatially deceptive
perplexing

Idea

Words generate mental images. In our work as designers, verbal presentation, argumentation, and convinction are essential. Our words also give form to the images in the minds of others. If we skilfully weave objectivity with emotional impressions, then we give expressive support to the ideas we have drafted. In order to communicate[G] coherently, we need a clarity of thought that helps us to organise information and discover or explain connections and contexts. A questionnaire consisting of five questions (dimensions) provides you with a structure with which to order observations and thoughts and evaluate them systematically.

Challenge

First, you should systematically analyse a typical work in such a way that you look at and describe one dimension at a time in a discrete sequence. Identify special details or combinations, analyse and specify them verbally. Select adjectives, nouns, or pairs of opposites (e.g. light-dark) and then categorise your observations in writing, assigning them to the following five dimensions:

1. **What does it look like?**
   Formal-Aesthetic Dimension
2. **What is it made of?**
   Material-Haptic Dimension
3. **How is it made?**
   Productive Dimension
4. **In what cultural context does it operate?**
   Cultural Dimension
5. **What relationships does it create?**
   Interactive Dimension

In specific terms, for all five dimensions you need to engage with the following aspects:

the Formal-Aesthetic Dimension includes form, colour, structure, proportions, and spatial dimensions. In the Material-Haptic Dimension, you note down the type and quality of the materials. You observe the properties and the special nature of the components. Is there a material concept? Then look at the Productive Dimension and examine the methodical and mechanical aspects. What production processes were used? What development process did the work go through? Is its quality the result of an artisanal process? What methods were used? With the help of the cultural dimension, you draw conclusions about the context and objective pursued by the project, while also organising meaning and symbolism, origin and genesis. In doing so, you undertake a critical examination of contexts. Finally, you analyse the effect of the work with the Interactive Dimension. You sound out actions and reactions. In this way, you check which interactions[G] and interpersonal relationships are generated by the work. You should (always) ask yourself this general question: Why is this special?

Finally, you identify connections and interactions between dimensions and categorise them. In the two subsequent phases of the method (experimentation and realisation) you will encounter the five dimensions again and with a different objective. Details of the dimensions will follow in chapter 5, (→ 41, 45, 49, 53, 57).

Not everything can be easily separated and assigned to the five dimensions – the world is too complex for that (which is a good thing). Use your own judgement to sort the design aspects. You alone know what they stand for. There is no "wrong" here, so be bold and keep your cool. In the next chapter you will reduce the profusion of words to a few keywords and visualise them so that they serve as a source of inspiration for your further work.

Objective

To articulate thought, we always need a form of language. You learn to interweave three things in one single process: visual information, your individual perception, and the written word. You will train your ability to associate and verbalise as a basis for communicative refinement with skilful argumentation. You will get to know the five dimensions as an analytical instrument to bring order to your own creative chaos later on. You will train your focus and use the dimensions to develop a clear understanding of the contexts and logic of various design factors. In this way you will develop a solid basis for assessing your own work (and that of others) in a reflective and transparent way. In the next step you create the basis for a visualisation matrix. The structuring of the information brings clarity, stability, and orientation into the process.

Words generate mental images.

3

Visualising and Abstracting

Interpreting keywords
The power of images

Scribble in your own
individual style, even
if drawing is not your
strength. Interpret a
motif (keyword) and
use objects to create
visualisations. Finish
by organising these
in an overview.

	scribbled	scribbled / graphic	graphic	three-dimensional / concrete

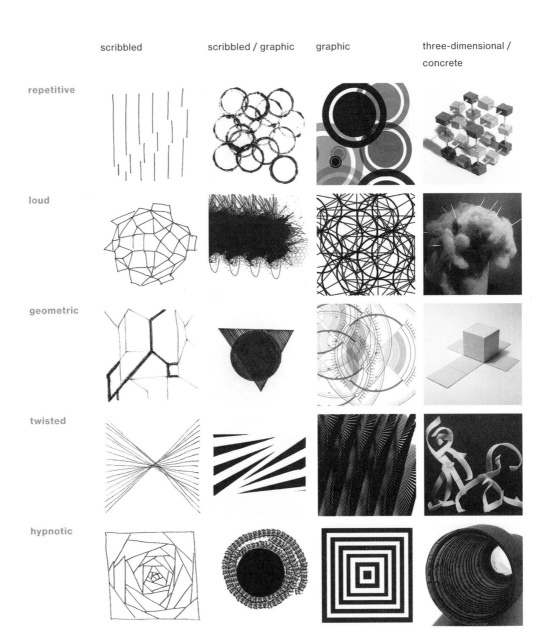

repetitive

loud

geometric

twisted

hypnotic

Idea

Images set energies loose. Visualisations are nothing other than representations that let us see a realm of possibility. Just as, while training for a marathon, we concentrate visually, intellectually, and emotionally on the upcoming event, we also create visual analogies to our thoughts in the act of drawing.

The visualisation chapter gives us scope to explore the possibilities of form and content in the design of our project. It begins with words, moves on to lines and surfaces, and continues into the space, with graphic and spatial interpretations based on the keywords. This creates an extensive collection of possibilities that you can pursue further. We use our own choice of tools to enable two- and three-dimensional representation, including pencils, brushes, digital tools, and everyday objects. You will get to know some of these approaches in a moment. Afterwards we get a visual overview of the material we have created with a matrix.

Challenge

Choose about 3–5 powerful keywords or simply your favorites from the previous notes you made when deconstructing your selected artwork and the context and scope of your project. A keyword can be a noun, a verb, or an adjective. It stand for a certain quality. Now visualise them. It is recommended that you take the keywords from at least two dimensions, with no more than two from the project context.

You can also imagine the conceptual level of the work you are analysing as a meta-level that resonates subconsciously. Keep your notes in case you want to use them again.

At this point, if not before, you will roll up your sleeves and pick up a pen, mouse, or needle and thread. And don't be afraid of the first mark you make. It is your view and your personal interpretation of a word, a keyword. An associative visualisation. It can also vary according to culture. I recommend starting with a pencil. It's up to you to determine the order in which you use your presentation methods. Generate the images yourself. Start with one word and if you jump between different words as you do it, that's fine. There is no "wrong" here either, so let's get going!

Two-dimensional – My friend the pen – Graphic and digital

With the pen as a medium, you delineate the word in graphic and abstract terms. Take advantage of the sense of liberation and ease that comes from knowing that the picture should not reflect reality in a natural way. In fact, a representational picture is the one thing you should not create. Find different analogous variants to illustrate a word. If you tend to work graphically in two dimensions, start in black and white, as it is the clearest form of two-dimensional communication. Use a ruler, compasses, stencils, glue, and black construction paper depending on the motif. Develop printing tools for pattern repeats, such as stamps, sponges, rollers, and brushes. You can use analogue drawings as starting points for digital visualisations. If you work digitally, play with the zoom or work with pictograms. Perhaps your ambition is to set only the minimum number of anchor points in Bézier curves[G]. Work first in greyscale, then in colour.

Material – From tangible to spatial

Have you ever absent-mindedly drawn a letter into the thick pumpkin soup in front of you and observed how the line slowly disappears again? Do something similar when you visualise your keywords spatially and in material form. The translation of the concepts into the material is a preliminary stage prior to experimenting in the laboratory and initiates the leap into three-dimensionality.
To do this, switch your workplace to analogue, go to the kitchen, the garden, or the workshop/lab. Go ahead and have fun, but don't do anything dangerous, especially when using equipment! It is recommended that you use

only one single material or a consistent combination of materials. This gives you a typology[G] that makes it easier for you to make comparisons, notice differences, and create new inspiring connections between the things you make. In Euclidean[G] terms, it is not difficult to step out of the flat surface. Your material pool is everyday life. Whether with Smarties, disposable rubber bands, paper clips, wax, paper, or bits of string – you can quickly produce visual results with almost anything around you. Then photograph your results consistently.

Create a summary and overview – The matrix.
The "matrix" in this method describes a tabular arrangement of visualisations. It serves you in three ways: firstly, it is the ordering system for an overview of what you have achieved so far. Secondly, it is your source of inspiration. Thirdly, the matrix becomes your visual reference. You will keep working with the keywords if you systematically link them to the five dimensions in the course of the project. The overview of the visual interpretations you have made serves as a creative reference and reminder.

For your matrix, first make a selection from the graphics you have created. Select square sections of the images. Arrange these in a table, with the vertical columns representing the manufacturing method. A quick look at the sample project on the previous page will help here. Reduce the size of the originals. Even if this gives them a different effect, don't let it put you off. It is important that you know what this picture stands for. Using an identical format of 5 × 5 cm (thumbnails or stamps) allows you to compare 2D and 3D visualisations and facilitates their interaction. Imagine the visualisations as metadata[G] organised in a framework[G]. Users generally don't pay attention to this data, but it will play a part in your project and stimulate you to create new mental connections. Finally, print your matrix on A3, tabloid-size paper and hang it somewhere prominent that you walk past on a regular basis.

Objective

Intensify your creative head-heart-hand connection and have the courage to implement your own ideas. The visualisation exercise will also increase your basic speed. With each experimental visualisation your repertoire grows. The more often you illustrate keywords with a pen in your hand, the more imaginative you will become.

Use defined lines, scribbles, and artistic representation in parallel. This trains your eye to see the essentials and helps develop formal decisiveness. By switching to a different form of presentation or reducing your palette to a few elements, you will learn to see the same content in different ways and vary it accordingly.

Starting from one word, you will develop an abstract spatial structure, which will stimulate transformative thinking. By working systematically from word to image, from word to material, and from image to space, you train your ability to read visualisations of any kind associatively and to represent spatiality in two dimensions. You will internalise this mental dissolution of surface and spatiality that is so important for creatives. You practise a particular way of looking at your ordinary environment, quickly repurposing things, as necessity is the mother of invention. You sort and cluster things in a considered way. Organising visuals helps you to grasp basic complex relationships more easily. You can also apply this principle in corporate design, if you choose to opt out of using the modular basic building blocks of font, colour, etc. You understand the advantages of standardising your image material when your sketches, schemata, pictograms, and visualisations are all on the same scale.

4
Grasping

Picking up, emulating, understanding

Idea

This module is optional, but helpful. It focuses on understanding through empathy. If all the dimensions and relevant contextual connections are already (completely) clear to you in your analysis of the work, please go on to the next chapter. If you want to understand an aspect of your analysis in more detail, I recommend this step.

If we look at the work of another creative person, we can generally access, via a process of creative empathy, an immediate understanding of the contexts in which their work arises on the basis of unlimited respect for intellectual property[G]. A legitimate step, especially to examine individual aspects more closely, is analytical empathy. You may have seen product designers at furniture trade fairs examining the joints under the tables to find out what construction solution was chosen.

Prior systematic analysis and research have enabled you to see your selected work through new eyes. This has brought new aspects into play that you can take up and pursue in your project.

You get to the bottom of things.

Challenge

Taking an active, spatial approach, try out one dimension of your selected work or a detail of it by tracking it exactly. Reverse-engineer[G] your work. First, observe the principles you encounter. Follow the rules of your chosen work and deduce your design or organisational decisions for a study.

Then grasp the dimensions (Formal-Aesthetic, Material-Haptic, Productive – methods and manufacturing processes – Cultural, Interactive) that you find exciting in your analysis and whose details you would like to understand more closely. Try to create something yourself under similar conditions. Research your own project by trying to "look underneath" it and understand it.

You can also do this on a different scale, work on a model[G], or switch to another medium in which you expect to gain valuable insights. It is definitely not about making a one-to-one copy.

Tip: With formal-aesthetic studies, you can quickly produce good results on paper. If it is the spatial experience that you want to reproduce, then I would still recommend a small model. If your focus is on the material that was used, work with it. If you are investigating an approach where different people were involved in the design process, try creating scenarios where you get feedback from others.

Objective

You will achieve a detailed understanding of individual design parameters, new insights, and expand your creative wealth of experience. You gently enter the realm of scientific experimentation, because you work with the intention of getting to the bottom of something. You will train your ability to transfer your discoveries if, for example, you reduce the scale, abstract the form, or change the medium. Designers regularly use changes in dimensions, material, and format in every phase of a design. In this step they generate models, three-dimensional sketches, and mock-ups[G] or paths. You train your openness to different sources of inspiration. Irrespective of the degree to which an artist is known, we can enjoy the mental kick we get out of their delightful solution. You can finish the Phase I "Analysing" process with a sense of satisfaction and pride.

If, after the first phase, you are bursting with ideas and everything is wonderful, then simply continue, with or without method. If you want to use the dimensions again in a different way, then get into the second phase – experimenting!

Experimenting

The second phase is conceived along the lines of a laboratory. In it, you explore and concretise components of your project. You collect and understand facts that define your project, and you study several ways of approaching things. The great potential of each of the five design dimensions is presented in the following chapters. In principle, all you do is develop a project experimentally. Simple as that. From the simple to the complex!

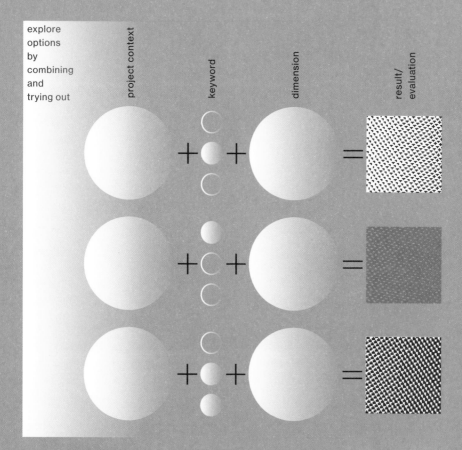

explore
options
by
combining
and
trying out

project context

keyword

dimension

result/
evaluation

become more
complex with
more dimensions

1   **Combining and Trying Out**
Combine your keywords
with the five dimensions and
carry out experiments in the
context of your project.

"At the beginning it was hard to imagine what experimenting with oils, corn starch, and butter could have to do with form finding and project design. But thinking through 'doing' and carrying out simple and inexpensive material testing is still one of my favourite design methods and a great way of generating as many ideas as possible."

JAN VEICHT, PRODUCT DESIGNER

"Experimenting with seemingly absurd ideas has led to a great project that we could not have developed without this phase."

TABEA ROCKE, INTERFACE DESIGNER

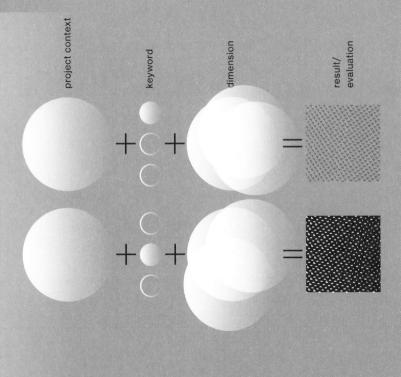

project context   keyword   dimension   result/ evaluation

link and
deepen
good results

2   **Connecting and Consolidating**
Link up several findings and special features from your experiments, drill deeper, and condense the knowledge into a consistent project.

Experimenting takes more time than analysing, but you learn to move with assurance through the five dimensions of design. If you approach it with the necessary openness, you will also reap the rewards.

5
Combining and Trying Out

Experimenting in the five dimensions
Scope, keywords, dimensions

Check possible combinations and try things out. Work from the simple to the complex. Experimental design can be messy.

Focus on the five dimensions in any order.

1. What could my project look like?
Formal-Aesthetic Dimension

2. What material could I make it from?
Material-Haptic Dimension

3. How could I produce my project?
Productive Dimension

4. What cultural setting should my project take place in?
Cultural Dimension

5. What relationships could it create?
Interactive Dimension

Idea

The best way to come up with a good idea is to generate an abundance of them. Ideas are intangible creative outputs. The challenge of this book is to describe the creative process in detail and to arouse and foster creativity so that it can thrive. Creativity arises in intermediate spaces and grey areas. This is where the method leads us. In these in-between spaces we are individual project moderators with full creative freedom. Inspiration cannot be provoked, but we can increase the likelihood of it occuring with the method described here. When you're combining, imagine you're clambering up a climbing or bouldering wall in a playful way. A lot of handholds in different colours and shapes are distributed irregularly on the wall. These correspond to the matrix terms and design dimensions of your project context. Climb up and test out all the possible combinations that can sustain and support you. At first you combine similar handholds, then you become more virtuoso and combine different colours with each other. You will most likely move upwards. In the book the climbing goes even further: when applying the method, you have Inspector Gadget telescopic arms and legs, which can also grab onto handholds that are further away.

General assignment in this chapter

Combine the keywords with the dimensions in your project context. Determine what is possible in each dimension. You may and should "go a bit crazy". The output may be – in fact, should be – completely unpredictable! You want to derive approaches for your own experimental series using associative combinations formulated from a keyword, a dimension and a project parameter. Stay cool, there is no right or wrong! Formulate the question for yourself: combining a quality [keyword] with your options/project context/parameters [scope]:

1. **What could my project look like?**
   Formal-Aesthetic Dimension
2. **What material could I make it from?**
   Material-Haptic Dimension
3. **How could I produce my project?**
   Productive Dimension
4. **What cultural setting should my project take place in?**
   Cultural Dimension
5. **What relationships could it create?**
   Interactive Dimension

Example:
If your key concept was [serial], your question could be:
In the context of my concept [serial] and parameter [working with paper], how could I produce my project [Productive Dimension]?
If you want to apply paint or colour, the possible production processes that you have in your armoury include brushing on, dyeing, spraying, and illuminating. In this step, you check the production process and choose embossing. You combine

the two and formulate an experiment on how you can achieve a colour gradation using an embossing process. In several studies you will try out different materials, embossing times, pressure applications, and preparations and find an intriguing approach that will achieve the desired result with several embossings. You try this out for the design of a book cover. You document the process photographically.

You've now charged the keywords with your own visualisations and ideas in order to use them as a source of inspiration. Please put the creative person you originally selected completely aside together with their work. The keywords and five dimensions from phases one and two act as your guide here. It's no longer a matter of just looking at the five dimensions but of working with them and within them. The next step is to examine them intellectually to determine their usefulness. If there are no contraindications, use them to develop something and then evaluate it. Do not immediately reject any peculiar intellectual connections, but consider whether they might have potential at second glance. If you have something that fascinates you, look into it. In return, be more tolerant elsewhere about ignoring a keyword combination. Go ahead! There's no way of getting it "wrong" here either. You are constantly working towards finding unusual solutions and not meticulously working through all the possibilities. You will certainly find a starting point. You are slowly orchestrating the project. The studies/experiments build on each other and the complexity increases (automatically).

A key rule in the chapter "Combining and Trying Out" is to work your way from the simple to the complex. The elements of chance, individuality, and meaning that yield results are central. Over the years, numerous studies have investigated how we can teach creative processes based on artificial intelligence (AI)

with the help of individual or machine learning[G]. The "problems" consist in creating analogies and finding the moment or establishing the relevance, determining which of the available experiments – yours, for example – has potential, and what selection to make to carry it forward. The second important rule is this: follow the exciting features that emerge during the making process, even if they are random by-products. You will enter into research-based learning and gain experience by doing. If the keywords lose their meaning over time, that's fine. The important thing is that you have come up with ideas. Experience shows that at the end of the project the keywords resonate somewhere.

Each experiment not only brings you one step closer to a solution, but also hones your "problem definition". In technical terms, you will practise empiricism[G], heuristics[G], and iteration[G], while working as a creative reflective practitioner[G].

You will most likely use several ways of working in the further development of your project. The experiment is the most important basic principle. Many of our creative ways of working take on an experimental character for short periods. Experimenting and inventing are closely related from a design point of view.[3] Act like innovators and use the experiment as a tool. You have to start a real project, now at the very latest – reading on its own won't get you anywhere.

Focus on one dimension in your project after the other as if all the other dimensions in the experiment were simply working up to this one dimension. The isolated combination and sounding out of individual dimensions in your project context serve as an orientation aid and protect you from arbitrariness. In reality, everything is interwoven. The clear separation gives you stability. Everything is very simple. To get under way, continue with work approaches/activities that you started with in "Material – From tangible to spatial". In the following chapters you will find a detailed list of the dimensional factors. If you are looking for a stimulus to get you started, pick a factor from this list. Document your studies. Please do not do this too meticulously, as this will kill the flow.

With each dimension you open a space and position your studies and the project within it, as if in a coordinate system. When you intensify your experiments, you usually combine two or more dimensions. It becomes multidimensional with overlapping dimensions. This is actually the next step (Combining and Trying Out). The shift is fluent and is described in the chapter Connecting and Consolidating. You don't need to carry out studies for every dimension, but you should think through all the dimensions until you have integrated them all. Now also take a look at Part C of the book (the picture section with principles and other projects). How intensively you work is up to you. You can never guarantee the perfect design idea. But the probability that the many combinations in your head will set off a creative firework is certainly very high.

Overall objective

In this section you will not only discover an eye for the unusual but you will also learn to break with habits and use them profitably for your projects.

Design can sometimes get dirty – indeed, it has to! You combine your senses, train your translation skills, and systematically fill your project with complexity. When you create new things yourself, you gradually gain control over all five design dimensions. You understand and determine every single dimension of your project and handle it with virtuosity. You work scientifically and creatively and generate a personal wealth of experience. You will learn to cope with the uncertainties of changing circumstances and influential factors. This dynamism is guaranteed in agencies, companies, and projects. Ultimately, you practice the "creative loop"[G] and the "mode change"[G].

Ideas are intangible

idea

creative outputs.

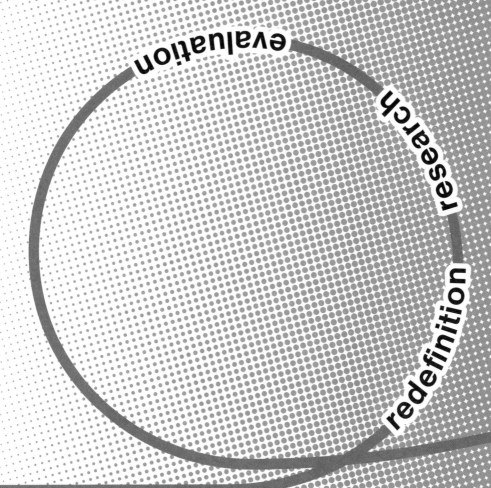

5.1
Combining and Trying Out
Experimenting in the Formal-Aesthetic Dimension

Look for aesthetic surprises and develop your own language of form.

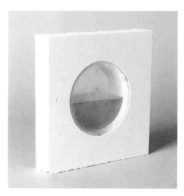

watercolour in a plastic box in plaster
[geometric] + [casting technique]

What could my project look like?

[Formal-Aesthetic Dimension]   +   **[keyword]**   +   **[scope]**

repetitive   casting technique
loud
geometric
twisted
hypnotic

plaster-coated spiral
[twisted] + [casting technique]

moulded spiral
[twisted] + [casting technique]

sugar crystals and food colour in an egg box
[hypnotic] + [casting technique]

Idea

When we create several variants of a shape, we use the various options available to us. We make fine and rough formal differences visible. In this way, we can fine-tune and adjust the aesthetic appearance.

Challenge

In the Formal-Aesthetic Dimension, you concentrate on developing a formal language and design details. The other four dimensions support you in these series of experiments to refine the aesthetic potential. Ask yourself the following questions: **How might my project look, what form might it take if I combined the quality [keyword] with my parameters/options/project context [scope] as a starting point?**

A brief example of the keyword [pointy], which you combine with your parameter [anything is possible] and the dimension [Formal-Aesthetic Dimension]. You ask yourself: What might my project look like if I combined [pointy] with [anything is possible] as a starting point? How can something colourful or a composition look pointy? You conduct a colour study, at the end of which magnetic paint pops up. It can be geared to "pointy".

Objective

You train the systematic creation of variants and work with different sizes, chromaticity, and shapes. In the course of this you will transfer a creative draft/sketch to different media.

Factors in the Formal-Aesthetic Dimension:

The structure (→ 190), the formal set-up. Analogue or algorithmically generative forms that emerge through growth. Diametrical, orthogonal, eccentric, equidistant composition through, for example, stacking, lining up, folding, fanning.

Geometries and mass. Diameters, radii, and angles. All possibilities of manipulating[G] them by rotating, fragmenting, or mirroring.

The composition, the spatial layout. The clustering or juxtaposition of things, playing with closeness and distance or the foreground-background relationship.

The free form.

The visual surface properties, illusion, perplexity.

Proportion. Anthropometric data or the golden ratio as a basis for measurement. It occurs more often in our culture than we think. Aesthetics in the sense of beauty.

The size, which can also change with respect to contrasts. In typography, for example, the font size and line spacing.

The dimensions 2-D/flat, 3-D/spatial, 4-D/interaction of space, time, and movement. Grids, repeats, formats, and layouts that emerge in the process of engaging with content are related to this.

The colour (→ 172): colour tone, brightness, and quality of the colour – for example, natural colours. Contrasts can intensify the tension (complementary contrast, quality contrast, colour-in-itself contrast, light-dark contrast). Wear and tear can cause gradations, gradients, or time-based changes.

5.2
Combining and Trying Out
Experimenting in the Material-Haptic Dimension

Test the possible materials that can be used for your project.

mirror pieces in plaster
[hypnotic] + [casting technique]

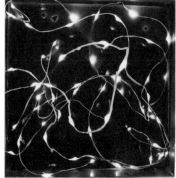

light chain cast in wax
[repetitive] + [casting technique]

What material could I make it from?

[Material-Haptic Dimension]	+	[keyword]	+	[scope]
		repetitive		casting technique
		loud		
		geometric		
		twisted		
		hypnotic		

light bulbs in plaster
[loud] + [casting technique]

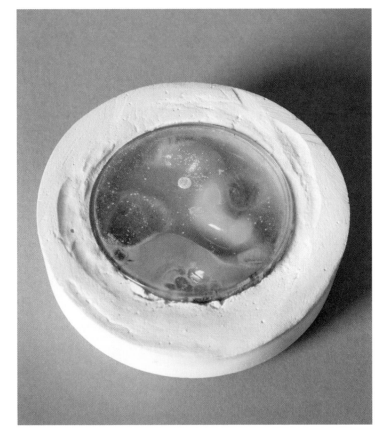

gummy bears (worms) in water in plaster
[twisted] + [casting technique]

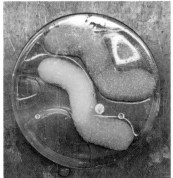

gummy bears (worms) in water
[twisted] + [casting technique]

Idea

Synaesthetes link impressions with sensations. Two simultaneous stimuli are coupled with each other. A great many synaesthetes work in creative fields. We design for and with as many senses as possible. We come into contact with materials and surfaces. Some of them smell, others give you goose bumps. By making a choice, we underscore our (own, creative) intention and introduce poetry into the project via the sensual materials.

Challenge

Develop approaches for a material concept in the Material-Haptic Dimension. If you don't have any specifications for materials, great, you are completely free in your choice of materiality! First examine any material in terms of its type, quality, property, and texture. Explore the context, potential, and effects of particular material combinations. Finally, focus on the following question: **What materials would I use for my project if I combined the quality [keyword] with my parameters/options/ project context [scope] as a starting point?**

Objective

You will learn how to profitably use haptics, tangible impulses, surface texture, and material properties for your project. In studying the materials, you will deepen your previous knowledge of materials science, sustainability, and sensory perception.

Factors in the Material-Haptic Dimension:

– Sensual material properties: the sound and smell or viscosity of a material. You can investigate to what extent a material influences sound and refracts light, or how you can use transparency. From a technical point of view, these are acoustic[G] and optical properties. I recommend that you let your individual awareness guide you.

– Technological, electrical, and physical material properties such as elasticity, flexibility, conductivity, or thermal behaviour. A flexible filament is shaped in 3D printing through a process of heating and cooling. Intelligent materials – also known as smart materials – respond independently to environmental influences. You can also knit in conductive threads.

– The history or future of the material: re- or upcycled materials or those which fit into the Cradle to Cradle[G] and circular economy principles.

– Ecological quality: here you can examine whether the material is ecological, flammable, prone to rust, coated, or biodegradable. Or whether it can get a nice patina and age gracefully. A material concept with the keyword "change" might target different appearances over time.

– The potential for connections appropriate to the material through positive locking, traction, or adhesive bonding. Positive locking connects things in such a way that they fit into each other like a puzzle, for example. With traction, pressure and friction are used for the connection, e.g. with a screw. An adhesive bond melts the material together, as in welding or vulcanising when you repair a bicycle inner tube. Since material and processing depend on each other, this is equally important in the Productive Dimension.

– Semi-finished products[G] as raw materials or the starting point for artefacts[G]: you can also consider semi-finished products as material. Things that might have a different future ahead of them. Everyday items are also at your disposal, in the sense of a raw material. Just make something new out of it! Example → 160

5.3
Combining and Trying Out
Experimenting in the Productive Dimension

You examine possible approaches – your special methodology within the method. You check machinery and manufacturing and production processes for your project.

How could I produce my project?

[Productive Dimension]   +   **[keyword]**   +   **[scope]**

repetitive   casting technique
loud
geometric
twisted
hypnotic

plaster and green food colour
[twisted] + [casting technique]

colour dripping experiments with
plaster
[loud] + [casting technique]

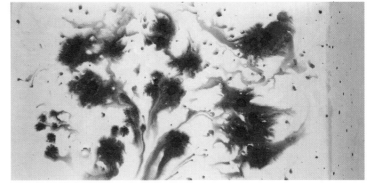

dried plaster with ink
[repetitive] + [casting technique]

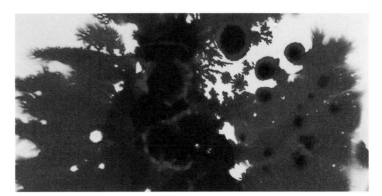

wet plaster with ink
[repetitive] + [casting technique]

Idea

In the experimental and creative process, designers and artists have always borrowed working methods from various disciplines. When we work, we always shape how we ourselves and others work. So the process itself is a product, and we can use it as a design tool. The questions of **how** something should be made and **by what means** it should be created can come into focus in the course of the drafting process. Different methods are all equally valid and can also be combined for our purposes.

Challenge

Explore the Productive Dimension with its (mechanical) production processes and possible development processes for your project design (and control). **How could I produce my project if I combined the quality [keyword] with my current framework/parameters/options/project context [scope] as a starting point?** Investigate and understand the functional principles of different methods and explore other ways of designing. Then embed the methods you choose in your project. Also research the production processes you want to use. Use your infrastructure! Don't be afraid of the first telephone call, and ask experts! You will soon become a specialist yourself and will be able to help others later.

Example: You have the keyword [angular]. You combine it with the Productive Dimension. You think about how you could produce something angular. An initial idea for mechanical production emerges: you could fold something (e.g. paper) or bend metal.

Objective

You get to know manufacturing possibilities, use workshops, read tutorials, and try things out. You will probably leave your comfort zone and communicate with experts. You try out ways of tackling projects from different angles, reflect on your methodical approach, and learn how to find your way around the spectrum of methods. In this way, you will develop a feeling for what approaches you like or what could be good for your projects in order to achieve the best possible results. As a result, you are already well prepared to take on a facilitator role as a designer in the future and will increasingly be in a position to design systems^G, (work) processes, procedures, and environments as commodities that enable others to develop things.

By opening and extending possibilities, by combining, restricting and defining variables, you confidently weave together the forms of divergent and convergent thinking that are responsible for creativity. At the same time, you create a range of things, such as questionnaires or material samples.

Factors in the Productive Dimension relating to working methods:

– Handcrafting with models and prototypes (also with digital concepts): Paper prototypes are a good intermediate step in the design of various interactions. The same applies to the Wizard of Oz principle (acting as if)[G].

– Mode change: Digital-analogue work and walking. Recommended.

– Self-observations and self-experiments: Use your own special knowledge painlessly.

– Observing, interviewing, or participant observation are scientific methods from qualitative social research and psychology. We designers use them frequently.

– Include expert opinions in your project. Enrich your project with the knowledge of others.

– Involve future users in the design process. A classic procedure in human-centred design[G].

– If, for example, you want to have people whose context you would like to learn more about photograph themselves in everyday life, you will obtain cultural probes[G]. This originated as an experimental artistic process.

– Field research, in which you explore the terrain in which and for which you design: It originally comes from ethnology and anthropology. Design thinking also makes use of these approaches. You can work qualitatively[G] or quantitatively[G].

– The principle of co-creation[G], in which the process of participating in your project is designed: Involving several people in your project allows it to grow into a joint undertaking.

– For very large projects, crowdsourcing, outsourced swarm intelligence.

Factors in the Productive Dimension relating to the production process (selection):

– Production in the sense of mechanical production: the treatment and processing of a material.

– Printing processes such as risography, letterpress, textile printing, or embossing.

– Additive production processes[G]: When the material falls onto the printing plate during 3D printing, this is also called offset.

– Machining processes in which material is removed by drilling or milling or mass is formed by shaping and casting.

– Cultures of repair, such as the Japanese *kintsugi,* in which the joints of ceramic fragments are gold-plated: no planned obsolescence[G] on economic grounds.

– Functionality and construction with details such as hinges or mechanisms.

– Integrate wind, weather, and sunlight as natural processes and let them work for you.

– Growth and construction processes of organisms (animals and plants): Explore these without doing any harm to them.

5.4

Combining and Trying Out

Experimenting in the Cultural Dimension

You reflect on the cultural context of your project in order to create something new in it. You can use the project to develop a critical attitude and deal with it constructively. The difference often lies in the detail.

"As critical designers, we are used to drawing other people's attention to negative aspects in order to change something in the world. We are so focused on the bad things that we often don't even consider pointing out the improvements. We have therefore set ourselves the goal of achieving some positive development. Many people think that the ozone layer is becoming thinner and thinner and that the hole in the ozone layer is spreading. However, exactly the opposite is the case. Political will makes a difference. After the completion of the global Montreal Protocol in 1987, which banned the use of chlorofluorocarbons (CFCs), significant improvements are now evident and the ozone layer is in the process of regenerating. In the Cultural Dimension the project "Dobson" was born, named after the unit of measurement that indicates the thickness of the ozone layer, we want to visualise both the current and the expected state of the ozone layer in the future. Based on scientific calculations of the ozone content of the next decades, we have developed the concept of visualising data via a spatial installation."

TABEA ROCKE, STUDENT

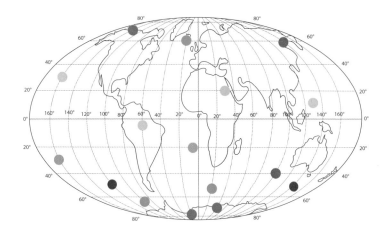

global ozone distribution in 2001

| Dobson units | <200 | 225 | 275 | 325 | 350 | 375 | 400 |

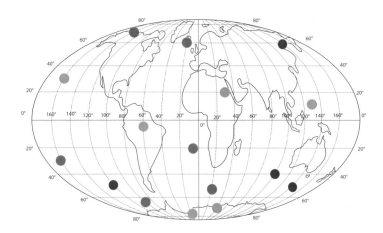

Expected global ozone distribution. A comparison of the two states clearly shows that the hole in the ozone layer has closed and that the ozone layer is slowly becoming thicker between latitudes 60 degrees north and 60 degrees south.

Idea

We always create something new against the background of a large cultural framework. Through our socialisation we bring our individual cultural background with us and act, shape, and measure our environment with our values. This is all wonderful and perfectly correct. Yet although our Cultural Dimension is often the most difficult to grasp, in our projects it becomes visible, palpable, and therefore essential. The sum of the details generates the cultural difference!

Objective

You sensitise yourself to the respectful treatment of foreign cultures as well as your own. You locate yourself, your way of thinking and acting, in a global context, through research and/or open discussions. Cultural and intercultural competence is an essential "soft skill" and highly relevant in social, political, and professional terms.

Challenge

Develop strategies and scope for interpretation in dealing with cultural assets for your project in the Cultural Dimension. Ask yourself, for example, how the topic is handled in a (different) cultural environment, what gestures, cultural codes[G], or behaviour you have recourse to. **In what cultural setting should my project be based? What statement could I make if I combined the quality [keyword] with my parameters/options/project context [scope] as a starting point?**
Use this dimension to clarify the conceptual level of your project. Develop ideas about your message and the intention you want to pursue. Write down everything in detail! Never stop questioning things. Develop an attitude!
Be critical and get out of your comfort zone. Question what already exists, pick up on complex problems and make them your focus. Social grievances are an issue in every culture (→ 170 Warm night). The Cultural Dimension thus also has explosive potential, which you can make use of for yourself.

The dimension is a hybrid, so consider the factors in the cultural dimension as suggestions, background information, and questions that should give you ideas.

— Cultural transformation[G] and changes in values: Scientists say that for about two hundred years we have been in a new era, the Anthropocene[G]. The technosphere[G] is growing daily. Make climate change or the Great Transformation[G] with scarcity of resources and digitisation your topic! Your visualisations and project can help shape the process of change (which is taking place anyway) in a positive way.

— Digital cultures, morality, and responsibility: What form of culture do we want with intelligent technologies? Good examples to the fore! What role do designers play in the current development of new technologies? Should designers really design backends that make reading data from the kids' room trendy? Get involved in the topic of machine learning, in which there are still massive biases with self-reinforcing negative effects in reality, since algorithms are based on the status quo. Or does the genie that's been let out of its bottle – artificial intelligence (AI) – inspire you to take a closer look at it?[4]

— You can use Critical Design[G] as a research method in designing.

— Storytelling[G]: What story do you tell? Stories and culture are closely related. Stories remain in people's minds and hearts.

— What prior knowledge do people have that you want to access? What discernment and literacy[G] do you encounter? Engaging with the theory of signs and scripts, with semiotics[G], goes all the way back to Aristotle. Look at the signs of other cultures! Make use of super-sign formation[G]!

— What collective visual memory[G] do you encounter with your target group?

— Culture of places: The genius loci[G] and all the factors that make a place unique. What is special about the atmosphere that only exists there in this form. Even against the background of globalisation, it is the details that are different on-site. A cultural mapping[G], a map that captures the cultural value of a thing or place, can be a good introduction. What (unspoken) rules or rituals are in place?

— Technical terms that you have already heard in the design context, for example what *wabi sabi* in Japan is all about: Reinterpret a traditional visual language[G] or let the material tell a special story.

— Corporate culture with mindfulness and public value[G]: Your project can become an idea for a start-up and you can be a front runner in the field. Reading matter on context and future: Florian Pfeffer's book *To Do: Die neue Rolle der Gestaltung in einer veränderten Welt.* "A tool for everyone who wants to change the world as a designer" (or with design).[5]

— The culture of togetherness: Use your personal cultural capital or collect it from others for your project. Learning cultural competence in theory is difficult. It is the product of personal experience. You only become aware of your own culture when you meet other people. Until then it is taken for granted. This is true in your own country and abroad. Travel!

5.5

Combining and Trying Out

Experimenting in the Interactive Dimension

You will explore the potential of the connections between place, time, and action. Investigate how people and things in your project interact with each other and the relationship between cause and effect.

Idea: A visitor picks something up, plays with the beautiful
movement of the liquid, then puts it down somewhere.

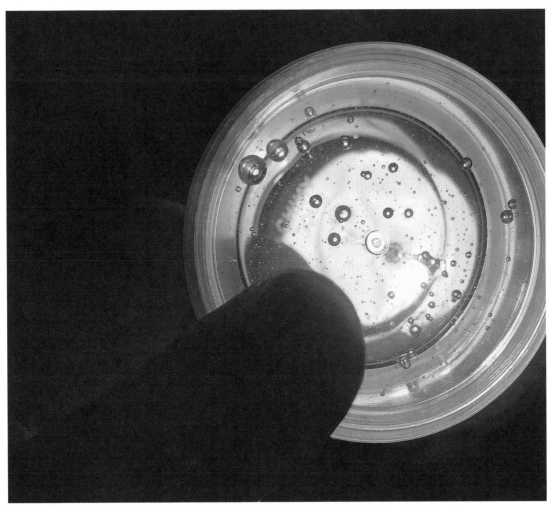

The fascinating movement of liquids is designed to get people to touch the object.

Idea

The Interactive Dimension is the most extensive, but not the most technical. Since interaction encompasses the interdependencies between people, machines, and our environment, the Interactive Dimension is at work in every project, because everything is related to everything else in our world. In this dimension, we investigate the analogue and digital activities that should or could take place between people and things and explore the relationship between place, time, and action.

Challenge

When experimenting in the Interactive Dimension, your goal is to develop (new) interactions. Determine levels of action. Create relationships, spatial effects, and points of physical contact that include technological interfaces^G. Focus on the benefits and effects of your project and the means by which you want to create them. This dimension can also help you develop the conceptual level of your project. Ask these questions: **What relationships could my project establish? What interactions could it generate/engender? What (re)actions might it trigger? What interaction could my project create if I combined the quality [keyword] with my current framework/parameters/options/project context [scope] as a starting point?**

Objective

Your perception of human, digital, and interactive influencing factors for design processes will become more acute. You build bridges between the digital and the analogue, dealing with cause and effect in an adept way and practising multisensory experience. You can explore anticipation^G and sensation. You will use your intuition^G to work out what we experience as an event with all our senses. You will understand why perception psychology is an important basis for multisensory brand management (including corporate scent and corporate sound).

The Interactive and Productive Dimensions are very close to one another at this point because they shape the user experience^G. Note: When designing systems and projects that are more closely interrelated, it is logical that multiple interactions are connected in parallel. In principle, then, the graphic elements below can have multiple allocations.

The designer designs a scarf that contains sensors giving the wearer feedback on the proportion of water in their sweat. The user is to receive this information acoustically.

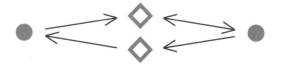

Alternative example: Grandma knitting a scarf for her grandchild, who is pleased with the gift and sends a thank-you card.

— The action levels, actions and reactions in all three interfaces (human-human, human-machine[G] and machine-machine): What happens how, when, with what, and where.

— Human-human: You create social interaction when actors interact with each other, e.g. by cooperating, initiating a dialogue, or communicating non-verbally. Example: Two people look at each other or shake hands in the usual ritual. Of course, we often communicate with the help of machines. Decide whether you are interested in forms of "direct contact", what role a medium plays, and to what extent it has a positive or negative influence on human-human interaction.

— Human-machine: the interaction with things. The medium with which you work is relevant for the interaction. The machine can be a piece of equipment, an object, or a mode of communication that acts as a medium or antagonist. According to Canadian media theorist Marshall McLuhan, the choice of technology, whether you're working on a book, a piece of clothing, or a digital artefact, is a message.

— Machine-machine: You investigate unusual possibilities for integrating your project into (higher-level) systems communication. Develop scenarios for a system like the IoT (Internet of Things)[G].

— The affordance[G] of a user interface: By inviting people to engage in physical or digital interaction in an intelligent, smart, and thoughtful way, you can enable people to act intuitively. Stimulate natural gestures in analogue and digital spaces[G].

— The person in the space: Create staged settings and encourage viewers to move through the space, for example to view an object from all sides. Communicate content playfully, publish in the space.

— Dimensioning: If you intend to trigger a certain feeling, the size and intensity of your object can play an essential role. Virtual reality[G] initially requires little space but conveys an intense visual spatial experience.

— The experience that you intend for yourself and others – the user experience. Technologies must adapt to us and not we to them. You simulate/sketch scenarios with real people or come up with personas[G].

— The cognitive knowledge (human factors[G]) that you can assume from your people in the project context: the mental proximity or distance, so to speak, to what you have planned.

— Spatial proximity and distance: We react strongly to the sense of touch, which allows us to feel pressure, physical contact, and vibration on the skin.

— The input-output principle[G]: An input into a (digital) interaction is followed by an output. This could also be a drawing. The output is always linked to the Productive Dimension, your resources and machines. The starting points for the development of your idea are the software, the process, and the end product.

— The hardware: The surface properties, haptics, and sensuality of a material can influence specific actions. (This is true too when reading an analogue book: How does the spine of the book sit in the hand? What sound do we hear when we turn the pages, and do we have a ribbon as a page marker?) Everything has an influence on how an artefact is perceived. Technical hardware can be sensors that measure oxygen content and/or temperature or react to the situation. Determine how your technology should deal with this information.

— The software: If you want to work and program digitally, you can design digital interfaces and presets[G]. The differences between similar software programs can be used creatively. (Example → 119)

6
Connecting and Consolidating

Fusion
Complex experiments

In studies and design approaches you relate the five dimensions in a controlled way.

Examining the translucency of various materials

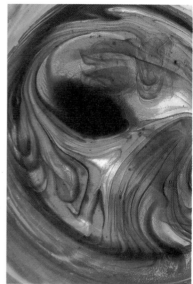

Shining through: stirring with light

Looking for the potential of cast-in liquids and their movement

top: water with ink, below: vodka with rasberry, gelatin, oil, ink and water, seeds, egg, honey, milk, glue

Colour series of water, honey, and ink

The viscosity and colours of honey with ink are investigated in more detail.

Idea

When we travel, we connect times, places, trains, flights, and luggage. We combine similarities and peculiarities. Combining the five dimensions is defined as an individual step in the method, even if the transition from simple to complex experimentation is natural and fluid. In your studies, drafts, and experiments you have explored possibilities in the project context. You specify the concrete contexts of your project and integrate all the dimensions. This step now brings you to the concretisation of your project, for which there are already exciting approaches, to be sure. New synergies and ideas emerge when you combine your experimental results, if you haven't already done so automatically.

Challenge

The project is becoming increasingly complex. Now take the test results from the five dimensions and prioritise them according to the qualities (and shortcomings) you identified in previous studies. Boost the dynamics with new combinations involving several dimensions at the same time. Continue to combine good results with other successful experiments and evaluate the results again. In this way, you intensify and gain ever greater control over the interaction between the dimensions. You then define precisely which combinations may be relevant for the success of the project.

Objective

The controlled composition of individual design parameters generates an increasingly complex series of experiments. You vary and adjust individual factors by systematically creating variants. This important component is helpful for project development processes and facilitates exchange with project partners. You will generate prototypes and train your ability to deal with uncertainty in the design process. Your individual stock of experience will grow, and you will become more confident.

If you've made it this far, you've already familiarised yourself with various topics in the previous steps. So you can rest assured that you already have a pretty considerable wealth of experience. Trust your gut when something is good or feels good.

Kill Your Darlings

In your project now is also the time to apply the "Kill Your Darlings" principle. If there was an experiment that was great but doesn't work well with the others, you probably need to shelve it for the rest of the project.

The "Kill Your Darlings" Principle: Are you stuck with a favorite design, layout, idea, or image and bogged down in the process? Then this principle applies: we sometimes have to painfully let go of these elements if we want to keep overall quality in mind. One indicator that you are stuck is that everything starts getting bent out of shape to cater to one object/idea/design, because this is the thing you like the most. But it doesn't quite fit. Unfortunately, it's a dead-end street, and you'll make better and quicker progess if you combine a number of other ideas. Be critical with yourself and see this step as a form of liberation. Despite the apparent loss, you're still a bit closer to a good design. Console yourself that the idea can be used in another project. You now conclude the phase of experimentation with a wealth of studies, evaluations, and new findings, and possibly some failed attempts and wonderful surprises too. You have drawn up a concrete plan for further action.

Realising

The third phase is that of synthesis. You develop the most complex part of your project by coordinating – while keeping your objective in mind – all the details relating to starting and finishing the production. In this phase, you hit the ground running and cross the finishing line. After that, don't sit down right away, but cool down a bit first.

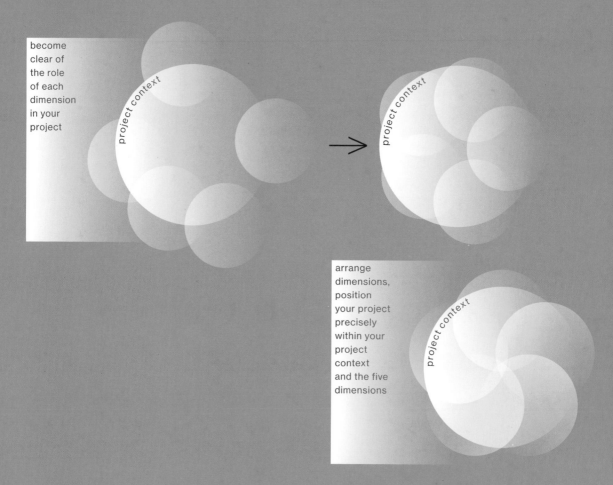

become clear of the role of each dimension in your project

project context

project context

arrange dimensions, position your project precisely within your project context and the five dimensions

project context

1   **Completing**
     You combine all your studies on the
     design dimensions of your project
     and implement your design.

"What fascinates me about the method is that it can be used not only for study or in the workshop format but also for creative projects of any kind and in a wide variety of design areas."

MAIKE PANZ, PRODUCT DESIGNER

"The method made me aware of how valuable analogue work and experimentation are and how, in combination with digital tools, they offer the greatest possible leeway in the form-finding process."

MAIKE PANZ, PRODUCT DESIGNER

"Thorough documentation has greatly facilitated decision making (in our team)."

TABEA ROCKE, INTERFACE DESIGNER

present

document and archive

2 **Presenting**
You communicate your idea. You prepare the content and organisation of your project.

3 **Documenting**
You keep an eye on the sustainable performance of your project and create a solid basis for this.

7
Completing

Executing
Implementing all dimensions

You work out your project in detail.

Final colour series with soap

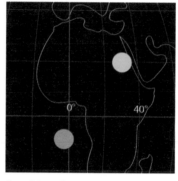
A world map is prepared for projection

LED lamps get cast in

You locate your project in the five dimensions.

1. This is how my project should look!
   Formal-Aesthetic Dimension

2. These are the materials it should be made of!
   Material-Haptic Dimension

3. This is how it should be made!
   Productive Dimension

4. This is the cultural environment
   my project will operate in!
   Cultural Dimension

5. These are the relationships it will create!
   Interactive Dimension

Each colour indicates a certain thickness of the ozone layer on the world map.

Idea

The machinery is up and running. This brings you to the third and final phase: realising. All the insights from your experiments are now synthesised. Synthesis is the antithesis of analysis. We don't do any dissecting here but rather bring things together. In this step, the sum of our creative decisions leads us to the product. At completion we are on the home straight (as with linear design processes[G]). You will now bring the five dimensions into alignment in a fine-tuning process. My mentor, the Italian architect Vico Magistretti, advised me to make project ideas so clear and pithy that I could explain them to someone on the phone, and they would quickly understand and even be able to implement them.

Challenge

Sprinting for the finish. Fine-tune all the dimensions with each other one last time. Go back over the five dimensions and use them as a checklist for the essentials. Check whether you can locate your project in the superimposed dimensions of reality or whether you can make the statements below. It's perfectly okay if one dimension is less well developed. This means that the project is focused elsewhere. All that's important is that you can locate your project in the dimensions yourself. Then possible adjustments will occur to you as you apply the finishing touches. The dimensions also provide an ideal structure for the presentation that follows in the next step.

You locate your project in the five dimensions.

1. **This is how my project should look!**
   Formal-Aesthetic Dimension
2. **These are the materials it should be made of!**
   Material-Haptic Dimension
3. **This is how it should be made!**
   Productive Dimension
4. **This is the cultural environment my project will operate in!**
   Cultural Dimension
5. **These are the relationships it will create!**
   Interactive Dimension

As you finish your project, you will come full circle to research again: finding out prices for materials or determining maximum sizes, perhaps. Because even during the fine-tuning and implementation process you will run into unknown quantities and new requirements. You will clarify these points confidently using the "information enrichment" process, which you are now well versed in. Imagine the creative process as a sequence of individual creative loops. As you work towards a goal, you move onward and upward. You augment your kinetic energy in the form of knowledge. When you reach the highest point, you have enough momentum to catapult yourself into the next loop.

In this step, your visual matrix comes into play again. You can consult your visualisations in making creative decisions. The matrix offers you a point of reference – for example, if you want to make a quick decision about arranging something. Use the ideas that you had at an earlier point in time.

Create the schedule for the final implementation, order the materials you need in larger quantities, commission companies, check tenders, and obtain feedback.

Objective

You transfer experiments and studies into a real project. As you organise and work on design details in parallel, you are training your time management and multitasking. Your discipline, the strength required to rigorously carry through a project, builds up your stamina, as you generate a functional project using the interplay of the five dimensions. This juggling will also make you more secure in all your future projects. Tip: Enjoy the buzz you feel when something is right. This is the moment you strive for when you work creatively. Give yourself due credit! The architects Herzog & de Meuron once said in an interview that these are the few instants of fulfilment that motivate us – this is what it's all for and you should really enjoy the moment. So, be happy about the good work you've already done!

Imagine the creative process as a sequence of individual creative loops.

8
Presenting

Planning, packaging, selling

You transform your project into a form of presentation.

View from outer space: In an interactive installation people place objects/lights on certain spots on a world map based on geodata. The colour of the light indicates the ozone thickness.

Idea

As soon as a project has reached a point where it can be presented, we transfer our creative work to the communicative process. Content and packaging are equal partners. We always create an ideal platform to showcase our project.

Challenge

Select your presentation format, based on what has the most potential for showing your work in the best light. Insert the project's core statements into this presentation format.

First ask yourself: How should my presentation proceed? How do I want to stage it? When choosing the medium, also consider external factors, such as the number of people you want to reach at the same time. Then set up specific logistics for the presentation date. By planning well in advance, you can free yourself from any last-minute stress and concentrate on the essentials, such as what you're going to say.

Objective

By transforming content into a new medium, you improve your ability to abstract. Depending on the format and nature of the end result, you make a video, an interactive installation, an intervention, a performance, a documentary video, an object, a series, a product. You will gain valuable experience in event management.

**I would like to give you the following pragmatic suggestions.
They can be individually adapted and supplemented for different events:**

Communication: Confirm the date. Invite guests if necessary. Organise any gifts for guests. Clarify the content of the announcements together with the partners or organisers. Get ready any media you would like to distribute at the event: for example, a summary booklet, your portfolio, or a short handout. Make sure you prepare the proper number of copies – and don't forget your business cards, if required!

Technology, equipment: Clarify what equipment the location has and what you may need in addition – for example, sound. Do you have wi-fi access and do your devices have the right adapters? Don't forget the charging cables! Can the room be darkened? What are the acoustics[G] like? Check any safety and security regulations! Save the presentation separately in the cloud[G]. Bring an additional PDF in reserve, as well as videos on a separate storage medium.

Think about who your audience is, how to pitch your talk in linguistic terms, what expressions and abbreviations are appropriate, who is on the jury, who you are competing against.

Arrival: Book tickets, check the parking facilities or public transport. Find out how you can transport any models you need.

Timetable: Coordinate the timings on the day or ask for a timetable showing your slot. As the host, you clarify the time, expected duration, and suitable hospitality to follow the presentations. Do not go hungry. Take something to drink with you or make drinks available.

Presentation: Make sure you rehearse several times. Make arrangements in your team about who will moderate. What kind of clothes are appropriate? Introduce yourself by name and maybe explain your function. Do not be afraid to create memo cards with key points. Be available for questions.

You know whether you are a designer with an eloquent streak or a salesman with a savvy pitch or both. You've already trained this aspect earlier in this book. Get advice or help from people around you who are even more effective presenters.

9
Documenting

Archiving
What's left
Next steps

You tidy up, file things away, prepare, and get the ball rolling.

Archiving the data for your portfolio

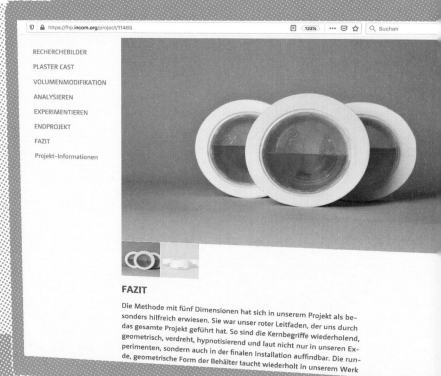

https://fhp.incom.org/project/11465   133%   ···   ☑ ☆   🔍 Suchen

RECHERCHEBILDER

PLASTER CAST

VOLUMENMODIFIKATION

ANALYSIEREN

EXPERIMENTIEREN

ENDPROJEKT

FAZIT

Projekt-Informationen

FAZIT

Die Methode mit fünf Dimensionen hat sich in unserem Projekt als besonders hilfreich erwiesen. Sie war unser roter Leitfaden, der uns durch das gesamte Projekt geführt hat. So sind die Kernbegriffe wiederholend, geometrisch, verdreht, hypnotisierend und laut nicht nur in unseren Experimenten, sondern auch in der finalen Installation auffindbar. Die runde, geometrische Form der Behälter taucht wiederholt in unserem Werk

Idea

Pooling all the relevant projects we've been involved in, we create a long-term record of our work and development. How we handle all the material also depends on what type of person we are. Some people find it easier than others to prioritise or to let go. We decide on the basis of individual criteria which things we choose to keep. Scientific collections follow special categorisations and are a fine source of inspiration for us creatives. In comparison, archives store material for an unlimited period of time and make it accessible to third parties. The intention here is to encourage you to thoroughly document your project.

Challenge

In this step you concentrate on the documentation of your project. Allow some time for this! Decide how the project should be preserved. You decide what your long-term aims are and work up the project for a new medium like your portfolio. Before disposing of or systematically weeding through project-specific documents, materials, or results, ask yourself how you can preserve the essence of them. Tidy up and create your digital and analogue project archive. Define an organisational principle. To do this, sort your data according to a logical folder structure and define a special location for notebooks, objects, and storage media. Write down the basics. You can write short project texts more quickly while you are still involved in the topic. Numbers and facts are all still at hand.

Style guides are available so that others can also work with typography, colours, grids, visual language, and layout. You don't have to create a style guide, but name files with the correct spelling so that you and others can find them later. Even the smallest typos can throw you completely off. Name files with year, month, day, title (211206_Inspired_by_Method) so that they sort themselves on the computer itself.

If your archive is a three-dimensional unique piece and you don't have the space to store it, you can rent a dry storage room. Check which things you can compress. It goes without saying that you can and should deal with objects in a different way than with a temporary installation, web-based products, or films. Your way of documenting your project and revising it for the archive will be as individual as the project itself. If you are not a skilled photographer yourself, be realistic about it and have professionals do the documentation. Is there a photographer in your network you can rely on? Give proper compensation for the service, because in many cases the pictures are all that will stay with you. Good photographers succeed in documenting and developing points of view together with you and in capturing your concept so that it is clearly identifiable in the image. Dialogue is essential here if you want to document a space. Be understanding if your 3D rendering is done from a point of view behind the wall, and you can't get this perspective[G] into the picture. You get a new angle with a GoPro or an aerial photograph. Build a network of people with whom you work well.

When making a photographic record of objects, make two variants where possible if you have not already done this while preparing the presentation. One should be a photographic staging in the spatial (usage) context; the other, a studio shot against a neutral background.

Map out how you anticipate using your material in the future. You don't need to create a complex marketing and communication strategy, but check your options. You can aim to submit your work to competitions, add images to your portfolio or website, or be pragmatic and keep them as internal references for other projects. Pantone Canvas is a database[G] and gallery at the same time. You can post projects there yourself and search for others based on specific colors. Adobe's Behance.net is an all-in-one creative tool: portfolio display, job portal, and with AdobeLive Channel, an entertaining format where other creatives can share their experience. You can watch them at work on the digital platform and gain insight into the different approaches colleagues take. Are you aspiring to take part in an exhibition, seeking to engage project partners, or looking to make a sale? Marketing experts will help you (in exchange for proper professional remuneration) in the long term with the launch or marketing of your project and increase your visibility. If you have an appetite for it, you can use growth hacking[G], though I would recommend sustainable, slow, and healthy growth processes. You can grant rights of use to your work to others for a fee; licenses are free of charge via Creative Commons[G]. If you want to give more depth to your project or initial ideas for a start-up, check the further financing. I have deliberately left the financial aspect out of the method manual but, of course, it always plays a role. It's hard work raising money with crowdfunding, but it makes projects possible that otherwise could not exist. Consider this as an option for the further development of your project, and support other projects! Simple ideas have already spawned large companies. Business modelling and entrepreneurship[G] are terms that you will encounter in this context. Work a little more on your objectives every day! Then you are guaranteed to grow well beyond your limits!

Objective

You will be sensitised to the relevance of keeping a record. As you explore the various possibilities of documentation and archiving and the choice between holding onto, sharing, and jettisoning (having weighed up your objectives and the possibilities of recycling), new material is developed and old material disposed of. This mostly visual resource will be useful to you later for talks, portfolios, or publications. Last but not least, you establish networking as a tool, because designers are always team players and networkers.

How we handle all the material also depends on what type of person we are.

Glossary

A

*Every time I have to look
up a word in the dictionary,
I'm delighted.*

—VIVIENNE WESTWOOD

Abductive
Working abductively means developing a general hypothesis/assumption from an individual observation. This process may involve experimentation.

Acoustics
"Acoustics is the branch of physics that deals with the study of all mechanical waves in gases, liquids, and solids including topics such as vibration, sound, ultrasound and infrasound."[6] Vocal pitch and breathing are relevant to making a presentation. Studies have shown that an audience adopts the breathing cycle of the presenter. When we are relaxed, our audience feels comfortable.

Additive manufacturing processes
In additive manufacturing, a material is applied layer by layer or cured to generate three-dimensional objects. Designers use it for rapid prototyping.

Affordance
"Affordance is a property or feature of an object which presents a prompt on what can be done with this object. [...] For example, when you see a door handle, it is a prompt you can use it to open the door. When you see a receiver icon, it gives you a hint you may click it to make a call. Affordances make our life easier as they support our successful interactions with the world of physical things and virtual objects."[7] The term was coined in 1979 by the psychologist James J. Gibson.[8] Jacques Tati's film *Mon Oncle* (F 1958) can be recommended as an entertaining classic about our belief in technology and interactions in the smart home.

Analysis
"Analysis is the process of breaking a complex topic or substance into smaller parts in order to gain a better understanding of it. The technique has been applied in the study of mathematics and logic since before Aristotle (384–322 B.C.)."[9]

Anthropocene
"The Anthropocene [...] is a proposed geological epoch dating from the commencement of significant human impact on Earth's geology and ecosystems, including, but not limited to, anthropogenic climate change."[10] The term was coined by Paul Crutzen in 2000, and in 2016 the International Geological Congress voted

to use this term. Humans have used the earth's resources for their own purposes and thus moulded humankind. The "archaeological" soil composition of the earth's surface has deposits from centuries of human use. The climate has undergone dramatic, adverse changes as a result of industrialisation.

Anticipation
"Anticipatory thinking (AT) is not trying to guess the future, it is trying to adapt to possible futures. It's about readying ourselves. And it's about guiding our attention – gambling with our attention based on what we are preparing ourselves to handle."[11] An anticipatory system is a predictive model. "In the context of ongoing events, the person uses his or her knowledge of and previous experience with similar events to generate anticipations of how ongoing events will unfold. These anticipations are continually compared with our sensations. Many anticipations are of a sort that manifest themselves as actions."[12]

Art
Art is the result of a creative process. It is "the expression or application of human creative skill and imagination, typically in a visual form such as painting or sculpture, producing works to be appreciated primarily for their beauty or emotional power."[13] Art originates in different formats and media, and the concept of art is constantly changing.

Artefacts
Artefacts are usually man-made things. But machines also generate artefacts – for example, in digital photography (pixel shifts when compressing JPEG) or in computer graphics. Although they are usually unwanted, they have great potential for inspiration.

Artificial intelligence
Artificial intelligence (AI) is a research subsection of computer science and deals with the automation of intelligent behaviour and machine learning. It was first developed as a field of study in 1956 by Marvin Lee Minksy and others at MIT (Massachusetts Institute of Technology, USA). AI, which Stephen Hawkins described as a genie that has escaped from its bottle,[14] is one of the driving forces behind the digital revolution. Weak AI is designed to support concrete application problems in human intelligence in specific areas, while Strong AI is supposed to be equivalent to a human's intellectual capability. "The appropriately programmed computer really is a mind."[15] Since there is currently no precise

definition of "intelligence" in this context, some researchers also speak of "artificial stupidity", because depending on how we define intelligence (social/emotional intelligence), rapid arithmetic and pattern recognition alone is not a sufficient sign of intelligence. The current discourse also revolves around the ethics of algorithms and AI-based innovations, the relevance of human emotional and social abilities, and the urgent need to strengthen social discourse around them. We need to talk about AI.

Association
Association is the connecting or linking of thoughts that come to your mind when you look at something. One thing leads to another.

B

Bézier curve
"A Bézier curve [...] is a parametric curve used in computer graphics and related fields. [...] In vector graphics, Bézier curves are used to model smooth curves that can be scaled indefinitely."[16] They allow you to work with few anchor points.

C

Cloud computing
"Cloud computing is the on-demand availability of computer system resources, especially data storage and computing power, without direct active management by the user. The term is generally used to describe data centers available to many users over the Internet."[17] Creatives in many cases use a set of applications and services from Adobe Systems, packaged in the Adobe Creative Cloud. Free alternatives for Adobe products are also available – e.g. Gravit.io and vectr.com (for Illustrator) or getpaint.net and gimp.org (for Photoshop).

Co-designing/Co-creation
Co-creation is the process of several people sharing in a design, i.e. collective design. It is currently becoming more popular due to social networking and the added value it is credited with bringing. Co-designing is expected to play an increasingly important role for designers in the next decades.

Collective visual memory
The collective visual memory is what the majority of people in a society remember of past events in the form of images of events. "We can also call the entry of an image into the collective memory 'iconisation'. It is the result of a longer process in which three aspects play a special role: stylisation, selection, and repetition."[18] I was born in the 1970s when colour film became widespread. My childhood was colourful, but many of my generation had the impression that their parents' childhood was black and white – as determined by the technology. Iconographic images from 11 September 2001 are in everyone's mind worldwide, whether they were experienced live or after the event. We are currently experiencing changes in the aesthetics of portraits with dronies (self-portraits with drones). They are changing our viewing habits and making the selfie look old. Charles and Ray Eames made the first visual dronie in 1977 with the film *Powers of Ten.*

Combination
"A joining or merging of different parts or qualities in which the component elements are individually distinct."[19] Fashion relies on combinations of clothes. In sport, different disciplines can be linked. In a swimrun, runners swim in sports shoes and run in swimwear.

Communication
"Communication (from Latin *communicare,* meaning "to share") is the act of conveying meanings [...] through the use of [...] signs, symbols, and semiotic rules."[20] The sender and recipient communicate consciously or unconsciously. We communicate not only with words and body language but also with the things we do or don't do and the way this occurs.

Context
Context is a general, personal, social, or linguistic context in which someone or something is involved. A so-called focal event (the phenomenon being contextualised) "cannot be properly understood [...] unless one looks beyond the event itself to other phenomena (for example cultural setting, speech situation, shared background assumptions)".[21]

Cradle to Cradle
"Cradle to Cradle® is a design concept inspired by nature, in which products are created according to the principles of an ideal circular economy."[22] The concept was developed by German chemist Michael Braungart in collaboration with American architect and designer William McDonough.

"It stands for innovation, quality as well as good design and describes the safe and potentially infinite use of materials in cycles."[23]

Creative Commons

Creative Commons is a global non-profit organisation that enables the sharing and reuse of creativity and knowledge through the provision of free, legal tools.[24] This means that other people can be granted the right to use materials for their own projects (music, films, images) free of charge. Seven categories are logically structured at CC and range from simple attribution to permission to make adaptations and distribute material freely.

Creative loop

The creative loop is a key element in the creative process. Having formulated and defined an idea, the loop takes us up and round through a process of research and evaluation into a new cycle of creativity (see figure ➔ 37).

Critical design

"Critical design uses speculative design proposals to challenge narrow assumptions, preconceptions and givens about the role products play in everyday life. It is more of an attitude than anything else, a position rather than a method." It is for "raising awareness, exposing assumptions, provoking action, sparking debate, even entertaining in an intellectual sort of way, like literature or film."[25] Anthony Dunne and Fiona Raby (Dunne & Raby) established this approach, which is particularly focused on design fiction and speculative design practices. The questioning and considered co-creation of digital changes is mainly the task of designers. The attitude it contains requires critical literacy, the ability to think critically and constructively. Let's never stop questioning things!

Cultural codes

"Broadly, a set of standardized or normative conventions, expectations, or signifying practices in a particular domain that would be familiar to members of a specific culture or subculture."[26] The origin and composition of a word (etymology) can also provide information about its meaning in a culture. When we develop a project in the East Asian context, we find different cultural codes operating than in the Western European cultural sphere. It is "read" differently than in Europe.

Cultural mapping

"Cultural mapping has been recognized by UNESCO as a crucial tool and technique in preserving the world's intangible and tangible cultural assets. [...] Collected data can be represented through a variety of formats like geographic maps, graphs, diagrams, aerial photographs, satellite-produced images, statistical databases, and others. From this, a comprehensive view of cultural resources can be stored and the documented data will serve as invaluable information for the development of national strategies that engage in accurate and sensitive analysis of people, places, and environments."[27] "Cultural mapping involves a community identifying and documenting local cultural resources."[28]

Cultural probes

A cultural probe is a design technique taken from the world of art. Usually, a kit consisting of a camera, questionnaires, a map, concrete instructions, and materials is handed out to a group of people (a special target or age group, current or future users) for them to record specific events, feelings, and interactions. After a preliminary talk, the recording process is followed by a follow-up talk and an evaluation. The aim is to obtain in-depth information and data on the living and working environment of these people and, more specifically, to record and understand the emotional and subjective value of things, thoughts, values, interactions, and rituals. These impressions will inspire and be reflected in the design.

Cultural transformation

In view of the scarcity of resources, urbanisation processes, and demographic change in society, there is an urgent need for action to change things. "Digital changes always have a global impact, so that global, rule- and fairness-based regulatory models are needed that enable a combination of digital and sustainability transformations."[29] The Goethe-Institut writes about changing values, political change, and sustainability: "Technical innovations and creativity are the most important resources for future viability. But technical innovations alone are by no means sufficient. [...] Art and aesthetics are of central significance here, since the transformation will not succeed by means of moral appeals, but only through a gradual re-colouring of our conceptual templates of quality of life and progress. We do not need renunciation, but higher demands in terms of our feeling for the aesthetic and ecological quality of landscapes, food and living spaces. We need a new ethics in the sense of an *aesthesis* of transformed perception. Here, art offers a fundamental education of the senses."[30]

D

Database

A database is an organised collection of data, generally stored and accessed electronically from a computer system.[31]

Deductive

Working deductively means basing one's actions on logical lines of reasoning.

Digital spaces

As with all growing technologies, augmented realities will be a broad field of activity for designers, even though there are currently hardly any prototyping tools for them. Dimensioning in digital and analogue spaces can also be used to regulate the spatial experience in an installation or scenography.

E

Empiricism

"Empirical research is research using empirical evidence. It is a way of gaining knowledge by means of direct and indirect observation or experience. [...] Research design varies by field and by the question being investigated. Many researchers combine qualitative and quantitative forms of analysis to better answer questions which cannot be studied in laboratory settings, particularly in the social sciences and in education."[32]

Entrepreneurship

"The capacity and willingness to develop, organize and manage a business venture along with any of its risks in order to make a profit. The most obvious example of entrepreneurship is the starting of new businesses."[33]

Euclid

"Euclid [is] the most prominent mathematician of Greco-Roman antiquity, best known for his treatise on geometry, the *Elements*."[34] Our understanding of geometric space is based on Euclid's fundamental laws. Space is a phenomenon with a topographic character, based on axioms of parallels and x, y, and z axes. According to Euclid, every three-dimensional phenomenon is based on a two-dimensional counterpart. The circle becomes a sphere, the square a cube, the triangle a tetrahedron, and so on. It is the same with organic forms. In so-called hybrid spaces, which we know from digital and cinematic worlds and animations – and which wander between the digital and the analogue[35] – it is possible to leverage these laws, and the spaces can change their dimensions.[36] If we work three-dimensionally, the mental step into the fourth dimension with space-time movement (and interaction) is less complicated.

Experiment

Many new standards and norms have been created through experiments. Experiments are the norms of tomorrow.[37]
Scientifically, an experiment is divided into these three phases:
1. Themes and anticipation (hypothesis): What topic do I want to tackle? What results do I expect to obtain? What exactly do I want to test?
2. Experimental set-up and execution: What material do I use? How much? What do I do with it and for how long? We qualify and quantify the ingredients and details of the execution.
3. Reflection and evaluation: What result did I obtain? What can I do differently, replace, or skip? Where does this lead me? The evaluation of and reflection on test series are important supports in developing design projects.

F

Framework

A framework is a scaffold or structure. The advantage of frameworks in programming is that they contain connectable components or standardised interfaces. A framework also implies structure, grid, raster, and method. As with Lego, the connectivity of building blocks can become a design feature.

G

Genius loci

The genius loci, also called the spirit of a place, is the sum of all factors that make a place unique: location, architectural and natural characteristics, and references to the local surroundings. The atmosphere in this place is not immediately measurable and visible. History and collective knowledge can also be part of the genius loci. If we respond to this and let ourselves be inspired by it, then it will become part

of our project or concept. Let us use the special qualities that only exist here in this form for our design and reasoning.

Growth hacking

Growth hacking is a (controversial) marketing technique. It was developed by start-ups and uses social media to maximise profits and to increase awareness. "Growth Hackers utilize analytical thinking, product engineering and creativity to significantly increase their company's core metric(s)."[38] This growth- and market-oriented technology also shows how easy it is to manipulate systems, unfortunately to the detriment of freedom of opinion. Algorithmically generated filter bubbles reinforce the impression we get from our exploration of the digital world. What is or would be important is that the logic of the algorithms is transparent. In the meantime, being on the move in the analogue world helps us experience everyday reality in its complexity.

H

Heuristics

"A heuristic technique [...] is any approach to problem solving or self-discovery that employs a practical method that is not guaranteed to be optimal, perfect or rational, but which is nevertheless sufficient for reaching an immediate, short-term goal."[39] "Eureka!" Heuristics is primarily an analytical procedure, a strategy of thinking, in order to be able to make statements and solve (complex) problems. One example of heuristics is the trial-and-error principle. Common sense, individual experience, and creativity are essential factors.
Researchers at MIT have always had a heuristic focus. In one study, they describe the invention of new solutions as a creative process of knowledge generation that is related to the iterative evaluation cycle. According to the study, successful inventors learn from their mistakes and overwrite past experiences and previous knowledge. They are open and intelligent and have high intrinsic motivation.[40]

Human-centred design (HCD)

"Human-centred design [...] is an approach to problem solving, commonly used in design and management frameworks that develops solutions to problems by involving the human perspective in all steps of the problem-solving process."[41] This involves

observing real people or developing fictitious personas and analysing their needs and fears. IDEO in San Francisco has been practising this successfully for decades. The IDEO Method Cards are highly recommended!

Human factors

Human factors describe the cognitive knowledge, social factors, and motor skills that we can assume from others, especially from our users. Visual ergonomics, for example, looks at how readable text is on a monitor or whether a certain typography is viable. These factors and the usability of an object or an interface are investigated in research by means of user studies or "usability testing". In 2010, the method was defined in the DIN standard (DIN EN ISO 9241-210) on the ergonomics of human-system interaction for the process of designing usable interactive systems: "Human-centred design is an approach to interactive systems development that aims to make systems usable and useful by focusing on the users, their needs and requirements."[42] The results are influenced by the performance, frustration tolerance, and motivation of those involved.

Human-machine interaction (or HCI = Human-computer interaction)

Human-human: Two people shake hands. Human-machine: There are two possibilities here. First, a person who shakes hands with a machine, which realises that it is confronted with a human who wants something and it must now react. Second, the machine that initiates interaction by shaking a human's hand, even before the person knew that they had any dealings with the machine. We know the principle of anticipation, i.e. what the person probably wants to do, from personalised purchase proposals by Amazon. Google has the patent on Pre-Order Shipping, whereby we get something even before we knew we needed it. We can send it back if we don't want it. This will be the next step ... all the way to "We'd better arrest you in advance, as you'll probably get violent shaking hands with machines ...". An algorithm-based pre-crime control program is already being tested by the German police in Augsburg.

I

Inductive

Working inductively means carrying out one's own research and deriving a theory from it oneself.

Input/output principle

The input/output principle is like a causal chain that switches between two states. In a binary bus, an incoming impulse (in zeros and ones) occurs, which emerges at the other end (in identical form) with almost no time delay. The input that our computer or microprocessor receives is usually converted with a piece of software. Before that, we determine what we (or others) do to get something as output. We may play music, speak, or swipe and this create an output somewhere else: a file opens, Siri searches for something on the Internet, parametric forms are created live to music, or the 3D printer prints. The input/output principle can be transferred to other things, scrutinised, and manipulated.

Intellectual property

"Intellectual property (IP) refers to creations of the mind, such as inventions; literary and artistic works; designs; and symbols, names and images used in commerce."[43] IP is protected in the German Basic Law, Article 14, and is included in Article 17 of the EU Charter of Fundamental Rights. "Intellectual property rights (IPR) protect a firm's intangible assets, allowing enterprises to profit from their creative and broadly innovative activities. Intangible assets account for more than half the value of companies and their importance is growing."[44]

Interaction

Interaction is about relationships. "Social interaction is a dynamic, changing sequence of social actions between individuals (or groups) who modify their actions and reactions due to the actions by their interaction partner(s). In other words they are events in which people attach meaning to a situation, interpret what others are meaning, and respond accordingly."[45] Social interactions can be accidental, repeated, regular, or regulated. In interactive media, interactivity may be defined as "when a message is related to a number of previous messages and to the relationship between them."[46]

Interface

Interfaces, be they digital or analogue, are points of intersection between objects, the surroundings, the space, and the human being. In architecture, interfaces are windows, entrances, and exits. Designers are always actively interfacing with existing creative professions and helping develop new areas. Interface and interaction design shapes the influence of the computer on our living environment and combines digital technologies with humanistic ideas.[47]

Intuition

Intuition is "the power of obtaining knowledge that cannot be acquired either by inference or observation, by reason or experience."[48] It is an aspect of creativity. Intuition arises from one's gut feeling and wealth of intelligent experience.

IoT

The Internet of Things is a vision for the future in which "intelligent devices learnt to think and goods could organize how to get to their destination all by themselves."[49] Each object is wrapped with a bit of software so that all the items can communicate with one another on their own. Forecasts say that 75 billion devices will be connected to the Internet by 2020. Perhaps this is also a reason for some of us to enter the world of programming, soldering, and cabling. Chain-linking interactive connections and algorithms is a complex procedure, e.g. when we visualise mobile geodata via tracking software in real time and this influences the design.

Iteration

"Iteration is the repetition of a process in order to generate a (possibly unbounded) sequence of outcomes. [...] Each repetition of the process is a single iteration, and the outcome of each iteration is then the starting point of the next iteration."[50] Designers always work iteratively. They conduct experiments in order to develop an approach, which they then evaluate. They might also test it and have it tested (its functional usage or how others perceive it) and then use it as orientation for the next experiment. Designers use the focused cognition that arises from this process.[51]

L

Lab

"The laboratory [...] is is a facility that provides controlled conditions in which scientific or technological research, experiments, and measurement may be performed."[52] It is used for monitoring processes and checking quality or for working on materials and manufacturing chemical products. Creatives use their workspaces for this purpose and for much more besides.

Linear project flow

A regular project in a design or architecture office runs in linear steps: briefing, rebriefing, basic evaluation, ideation/preliminary concept, concept with cost estimate, prototyping, draft with cost calculation, approval planning, execution/final artwork/lithography/ pre-press, tendering procedure, production/programming/implementation, documentation.

Literacy

Literacy denotes the ability to read and write. It covers the sum of our experience and basic skills related to narrative, linguistic, and written culture: text comprehension, semantic understanding, linguistic abstraction, familiarity with written language, and the ability to express oneself in writing.[53] "Digital literacy refers to an individual's ability to find, evaluate, and compose clear information through writing and other mediums on various digital platforms."[54] It is important to know and exchange ideas about the narrative, linguistic, and written culture – digital and analogue – of your readers, users, or project partners. Images, typography, and patterns are read very differently in Western European culture than they are in the East. If you speak several languages, you will convey words and the differences in their emphasis and contextualisation into another culture. The optimum approach is for us to be routinely fascinated by the shifting meaning of individual words. If we take typesetting as an example, we find the word "furniture" used to describe pieces of wood that serve to correctly position and space the characters in a letterpress chase. In this way, the individual letters find themselves comfortably "furnished". Critical literacy[G] is becoming increasingly relevant, the ability to question existing set-ups and facts, classify them, and assess them in a sound way. In particular, universities have the responsibility to educate future decision-makers in society to become critical and open-minded characters with the ability to make competent judgements.[55]

M

Machine learning

Machine learning describes the "artificial" generation of knowledge from experience: an artificial system not only learns "by rote" from examples but can generalise them after the learning phase has ended. It recognises and combines patterns and basic principles in/from the learning data.

Manipulation

Manipulation is the skilful modification and influencing of a state or process in an unforeseen way.

Metadata

"Metadata describes other data. It provides information about a certain item's content. For example, an image may include metadata that describes how large the picture is, the color depth, the image resolution, when the image was created, and other data."[56]

Methods

A method (Greek *méthodos,* "pursuit of knowledge") "a particular procedure for accomplishing or approaching something, especially a systematic or established one".[57]
It is a normally progressive procedure for achieving goals. These can be scientific findings or practical results. Methods are used in all areas of life, from everyday life to art, philosophy, and across the sciences. (Essay on methods → 100)

Mock-up

"In manufacturing and design, a mockup, or mock-up, is a scale or full-size model of a design or device, used for teaching, demonstration, design evaluation, promotion, and other purposes."[58]

Mode change

"Mode change" is a method to maintain flow in creative work. If a project is unable to move forward, then this is a good time to interrupt our current course of action. Once we have produced a sketch, we go to the workshop and construct a dummy or model, for example. If we have just come up with a draft concept, we go out for a walk and clear our heads.

Model

A model is a simplified representation of reality. We can use it to simplify sensual and visual things as well as theories. According to Herbert Stachowiak, a model is characterised by at least three characteristics: it represents "something", captures the most relevant attributes of the original, and has a pragmatic character.[59]

O

Obsolescence

"Obsolescence is the state of being which occurs when an object, service, or practice is no longer wanted even though it may still be in good working order."[60] Planned obsolescence is usually not sustainable. Smartphone manufacturers or digital service providers use it to maximise profits by making software and hardware incompatible and impossible or expensive to repair. Temporary tattoos, water-soluble materials, or edible paper are a good starting point for planned obsolescence.

P

Parameter

Parameters are (measurable) factors that make it possible to monitor and compare results in a comprehensible way and to create series and variables. In music they "denote acoustic variables such as pitch, rhythm, volume, and harmonics."[61]

Perception

Perception is the interaction between the mind and the environment. Sensual perception classically refers to the reception of events through seeing, hearing, tasting, smelling, and touching. It is an active process in which man interacts with his environment. The philosopher Alva Noë describes perception as a dynamic interaction between our brains, our minds, our surroundings, and other people.[62] "Consciousness is not like digestion, something that happens in us in a particular part of the body. It's something we do."[63] Haptic perception is "literally the ability 'to grasp something'. Perception in this case is achieved through the active exploration of surfaces and objects by a moving subject, as opposed to passive contact by a static subject during *tactile perception.*"[64] Braille acts as haptic, tactile, materialised

typography. In design we always ask ourselves: Who will touch (emotionally or physically) what? Where, in what way, with what, and how does she or he touch it? What does this trigger?

Personas

Personas are a range of imaginary human prototypes with concrete characteristics and certain behaviours who operate or need something. Designers use them to play through scenarios. A scenario can be a user journey in which all points of contact with a service, a brand, or an event are examined in a chronological sequence. Methods from psychology and market research, such as the development of personas, milieu studies, and target group definition, are used to support design processes.

Perspective

Perspective defines the distance between space, object, and observer. It also describes the angle from which something is viewed or documented. We can efficiently use a change of perspective in illustrations. We use it to create impressive images and can use distortions in composition. The view from ground level is dramatic, while the bird's-eye view is clearer.

Pictogram

"A pictogram, also called [...] an icon, is an ideogram that conveys its meaning through its pictorial resemblance to a physical object."[65] The pictograms of the 1972 Olympic Games in Munich by Otl Aicher, who was inspired by Otto Neurath, were pioneering. Pictographic representations are useful if we want to describe a procedure.

Presets

"A preset may refer to [...] a setting or value automatically assigned to a software application, computer program," or "pre-programmed setting on various electronic products and musical instruments."[66]
If we are the creator/programmer of a software interface, we anticipate possible configurations and menu selections. For the convenience of the user, we can create presets. We can, as it were, put the Spaghetti Ice Cream option on the menu, because we know that vanilla ice cream with strawberry sauce goes down well. When designing an orientation navigation system, the first thing to do is to find several possible solutions. A person's actions are as individual as the person himself. We can use prototypes and iterative feedback loops to approximate the desired reaction/action we want to evoke.

Process

A process is a "sequence of interdependent and linked procedures which, at every stage, consume one or more resources (employee time, energy, machines, money) to convert inputs (data, material, parts, etc.) into outputs. These outputs then serve as inputs for the next stage until a known goal or end result is reached."[67]

Public value

Public value describes "the value that an organization contributes to society. The term was originally coined by Harvard professor Mark H. Moore who saw it as the equivalent of shareholder value in public management."[68] "Value" creation is only guaranteed when the benefit is valued and socially accepted. Public value can be regarded as a positive trend. The iF (international forum) awards prices for this every year. In his manifesto "How Designers Can Change the World", Mauro Porcini, Chief Design Officer at Pepsico proposes thinking holistically and acting in the public interest. Responsible creative people and designers have been brought onto company boards, while Berlin is also seeing the emergence of "conscious businesses", start-ups with a mindful attitude.

Qualitative

This has to do with the quality of something. We work qualitatively (something that tends to be unclear in purely numerical terms) with open questions in an interview or a participatory observation. In the process we collect impressions and direct quotes. Thoroughly researched Facebook groups open up avenues of contact with specialists in all kinds of areas and lead us to new horizons. The measuring tools, instruments, questionnaires, markers, etc. also influence the result. How we ask questions and how we let study participants construe things, mark, or make a cross, the choice of pens, readability or graphics always have an effect. Qualitative data collection can tip the scales in major decision-making processes, such as urban planning.[69]

Quantitative

This has to do with the amount of something. If we measure a (large) number of things and evaluate the results statistically, perhaps also visualise them as graphics, then we work quantitatively (while largely neglecting the ambient quality). We can define the standard or norm upon which our measurements are based. It should be transparent and comprehensible. SurveyMonkey.de and LamaPoll.de offer free surveys. The open-source monitoring platform Prometheus.io is ideal for collecting and managing large amounts of data.

Reasoning

Good argumentation combines logical thinking with resilient reasoning.[70] It supports us in expressing an opinion. Visual reasoning is thinking in pictures. Statements are not constructed illustratively by imaging techniques but are equivalent to language.

Reflective practitioner

In practice, the term "reflective practitioner" is also comparable to the principle of learning by doing. It was developed by the philosopher and MIT design researcher Donald Schön. It describes the reflection of creators in action. According to Schön, our knowledge lies in action, and action creates knowledge. He defines three types of action: knowing-in-action, reflection-in-action, and reflection-on-action.[71]

Research

Research is "the systematic investigation into and study of materials and sources in order to establish facts and reach new conclusions."[72] It is vital in making progress in the creative process. For designers, research is an obvious way of enhancing knowledge. In-depth information underpins clarity, providing a solid foundation and orientation in the process. The browser extension Onetab is a freeware helper that provides a good overview.

Reverse engineering

Reverse engineering involves tracing the origins of an object or product in order to understand the process of its creation.

Semi-finished products

Semi-finished products (also known as intermediate goods or producer goods) are "used as inputs in the production of other goods including final goods. [...] In the production process, intermediate goods either become part of the final product, or are changed beyond recognition in the process."[73]

Semiotics

Semiotics, sometimes also called sign theory, is "the study of sign process (semiosis), which is any form of activity, conduct, or any process that involves signs, including the production of meaning."[74] Semantics, a subdomain of semiotics, is the study of the meaning of signs of all kinds.

Service design

"Service design is the activity of planning and organizing [the] people, infrastructure, communication and material components of a service in order to improve its quality and the interaction between the service provider and its customers."[75]

Storytelling

Storytelling is a tried-and-trusted method of communicating content emotionally. It can also reinforce brand recognition for a specific target group. Stories make something sympathetic, approachable, and credible, leading to a closer sense of identification, because you can understand its context or provenance.

Strategy

In business, strategy is "a method or plan chosen to bring about a desired future, such as achievement of a goal or solution to a problem".[76] It is used to plan the development of a project (or company). A corporate design sets out to create an important strategic tool for branding a company. As a general rule, the concept, the conceptual framework of the project, goes hand in hand with a strategy.

Super-signs

Super-signs are condensed information, a combination of elementary signs assembled in our consciousness into a new entity composed of complexes, classes, and relations. You show a portion of something, and this information is sufficient for the brain to think the rest. Try it with an apple. It is enough for us to see half a tiger in the jungle to know that we must run (or be eaten).

Synthesis

Synthesis is "the combination of components or elements to form a connected whole."[77]
In contrast to cotton, humans determine the material properties of synthetic fibres. The molecules are connected to become polymer chains. Now you can weave your individually tailored project according to this principle.

System

The system (ancient Greek *sústēma*, "a whole composed of several individual parts") is generally defined as a set of elements which are interconnected and can therefore be regarded as a single unit. "A system is delineated by its spatial and temporal boundaries, surrounded and influenced by its environment, described by its structure and purpose and expressed in its functioning."[78] We design ecological, natural, or artificial systems.

T

Technosphere

The technosphere is a culture-dependent earth sphere, in contrast to the natural sphere. It includes large systems for energy and resource extraction, power supply, communications, transportation, finance and other networks, governments and bureaucracies, large plantations, and cities as well as parts of them such as windows. If they were gone today, we would be in the Stone Age immediately.[79]

Transformation

Transformation is the process of changing a state. States can switch: from liquid to solid and gaseous, from real to fictitious and visionary, from spatial to planar and mental.

Typology

A typology is a classification of content or things based on certain properties. We can extrapolate from the individual to the whole or from the general to the specific.

U

User experience

User experience refers to our immediate experience and the experience beyond that. According to Don Norman, who coined the term user experience (UX), this is "the way you experience the world, it's the way you experience your life, it's the way you experience a service or an app or a computer system".[80] Interaction Design (IxD) is the "practice of designing interactive digital products, environments, systems, and services".[81] Design acts as a "subtle stage set for an action performance".[82] The term "interaction" and its interpretation change dynamically like the concept of art. Service design is dedicated to the optimal and ideally meaningful points of contact and processes of people and machines (as well as brands).

V

Virtuality

Virtuality, as conceived by the philosopher Gilles Deleuze, refers to "an aspect of reality that is ideal, but nonetheless real".[83] In the ordinary sense, it is "the quality of having the attributes of something without sharing its (real or imagined) physical form"[84] (see also Digital spaces). Virtual reality, VR for short, is "a simulated experience that can be similar to or completely different from the real world".[85] VR glasses can be used to create immersive and multisensory experiences. In doing so, we leave the real space with our senses, while the rest of us remains behind.

Visual

A visual is "a picture, piece of film, or display used to illustrate or accompany something."[86]

Visualisation

Visualisation is the analogue, media-based, or mental creation of images. These usually serve for communication purposes and to depict content. They are used in the natural sciences, psychology, design, and many other fields to illustrate, tell, convey, clarify, or represent. Visualisations can be two-, three-, or multi-dimensional. (Tips on 3D visualisations → 99.)

Visual language

Visual language encompasses the possible connotations of the content, the structure, and the formal aspects of a picture. In corporate design, a so-called "look" is defined for motifs in a series of images.

Wizard-of-Oz experiment

A Wizard of Oz experiment is the term used in the field of human-computer interaction to refer to "a research experiment in which subjects interact with a computer system that subjects believe to be autonomous, but which is actually being operated or partially operated by an unseen human being."[87]
Here's an example: someone sits in a box. On the outside, someone else presses a painted button and something happens. My colleague Walter Hardt developed the first ATM with this prototyping principle for and with Siemens Nixdorf in the late 1970s.

Mini class on perception:
With five-finger exercises to train perception, organisational principles, and much more, you can enhance your skills 24/7 and independently of your project. Please do them any time you like as a relaxation exercise! Further suggestions on the kind of project you can actually tackle can also be found here. (How can I try out the method? → 95)

Five-finger exercises

Tapas for in-between moments

In this part of the book you will find exercises that you can use immediately to relax your mind. You transfer basic principles of individual work steps from section A (the method description) into the everyday environment.
Have fun!

1

Selection criteria

Every day we unconsciously select things and make decisions every minute. For this exercise, I ask you to remember the last time you went grocery shopping. How do you choose the products that end up in your basket? Is price a critical factor, do you prefer organic products, or do you always rely on tried-and-tested products? Do you proceed systematically or spontaneously? Write down the criteria that played a role. Apply three of your criteria to the selection of a font for the design of a receipt. (Analysing ▶ Selecting)

10 min.

2

Navigating using voice commands
(1–4 persons)
Imagine two or more people navigating through a space exploring the precision and interaction of information. The basic principle is used in autonomous driving and in the design of interfaces. There are two different roles. One acts as a guide and speaks in a loud voice, while the others walk and translate the words into actions. Only use announcements, singly and in combinations that have been agreed in advance: Right, left, stop, 30 degrees, 45 degrees, 60 degrees, 90 degrees. Observe a variety of how the guided ones interpret the same command. Instructions like open the door, climb the stairs, bend down are disregarded. It's about directional turn-by-turn navigation based on speech recognition. The people taking directions have their eyes open. Work out the angles (How far do I turn for 30 degrees?) and the speed in advance and get yourselves in sync. Then swap roles. Keep the destination secret. An outdoor route or walking through large rooms is particularly suitable for this. You can also do the exercise on your own and try to give yourself instructions before performing certain actions. In this way, going to the toilet becomes a parking manoeuvre. (Analysing ▶ Describing)

5 min.

3

Describing sound patterns

For ten minutes, concentrate exclusively on what you hear. This works best in situations where you can close your eyes. For example, on a park bench or during a long train journey. There is the rustling of paper when your neighbour reads his newspaper or the sound of nylon straps on a backpack. Have your pen and notebook ready to document your experiences. You will find that you automatically search for the right words, and new pictures will appear in your head ... (Analysing ▶ Describing)

10 min.

4

Analysing proximity and distance

The law of proximity lets us read. We associate letters that are closer to each other. Distances create spaces. The alignment of volumes and elements defines their relationship to each other and creates a composition. Analyse your own environment according to organisational principles. It's also an intriguing exercise in public space, on the train, and in shops. Who is facing whom? How are the chairs arranged? What kind of seating area do they produce? And how are the magazines laid out on the shelves? For 10 minutes at a location of your choice, look with an analytical eye exclusively through the "distance and alignment glasses". (Analysing)

10 min.

5

Letter to Granny

In this exercise, you imagine a conversation with a person who is not familiar with the subject. How would you describe the project or the facts to this "outsider"? What are the relevant facts that this person needs to know? Explain the current state of your project in simple words. Apply this to one of the next challenges you're currently facing. Write it down or speak out loud on your own as if you were having a conversation. This will enable you to step out of yourself. (Analysing ▶ Describing)

15 min.

6

Organisational principles
Tidy house, tidy mind

How are the clothes in your wardrobe sorted? By colour? Try rearranging it sometime! Focus in on the fabrics: Are there any similar features in the materials your clothes are made of? Are there clothes that can only be worn at certain times of the year or could you sort them by outfit? Do the sorting process once and look at the changes. (Analysing ▶ Sorting and Evaluating)

20 min.

7

The Cape of Good Design, (aka Designers of the Carribean)

Draw your project as a topographic map, treasure map, city map, or world map. Identify elements of your project as continents, islands, countries, regions, capitals, mountains, plateaus, valleys, coasts, bays, seas, rivers, and deltas. What are the relationships (between them)? How did you visually sort your project? What priorities and relationships become visible? (Analysing ▶ Sorting and Evaluating)

15 min.–5 h.

8

Visualising with a collage

Now try using collage as a way to represent a chronological sequence! Illustrate your typical working day or just a day taken at random. Catalogue your activities and make a route map. For your collage you can use pictures from a magazine, your own sketches, or receipts from the supermarket. Put in a new format, a day can appear in a completely different light. Playing with size and layout can shift temporal perspective.
(Analysing ▶ Visualising)

30 min.

9

Four warm-up drawings

Take a pen of your choice and sketch someone's portrait for 5 minutes at a time. Vary the sitting posture and view. Maybe you also take turns? Or choose an object instead. It's not about making an exact reproduction, it's about developing a sense of how a line is created on paper and how visual perception and the motor skills in your own hand are linked.

One-line drawing: You start at any point and don't stop the pen the whole time you're drawing. You'll end up with double lines, gaps, and a very special style.

Blind drawing: You portray the person without looking at the paper. Don't cheat! It works and gets you in the mood.

Drawing with a different hand: Now take the pen in the hand you don't usually draw with. Don't worry – with a little practice you'll become a drawing ace. Aircraft pilots need to be nimble-fingered and completely ambidextrous. And even if you don't manage, enjoy the ride. You're not building an airplane and you don't have to fly it!

Drawing a blank: Choose an object that contains some empty space, such as a chair. Describe the chair in graphic terms by visually latching on to the negative space around and inside the object. The shape of the chair will be created automatically.
(Analysing ▶ Visualising)

20 min.

10

Infographics in everyday life

On your marks, get set, go! Write a to-do list or shopping list without using words. Use icons and illustrations. How do you represent a bottle of wine without words? For example, how do you show your favorite type of grape?
(Analysing ▶ Visualising)

10 min.

11

Don't Mind the Gap!
Two-dimensional visualisation

For this exercise we move into the field of typography. Choose a text of your choice, with letters that are as large as possible. This can be from a daily newspaper, some old notes, etc. In the second step, you build a small passe-partout that shows about three letters. You use this as a viewfinder. Now use this to find exciting extracts in your text. The idea is to look only at the shapes and not at the letters. In the next step, enlarge some of the areas as drawings on a sheet of A4. In the final step, invert the found shape and look at the spaces you have just created.
(Analysing ▶ Visualising)

30 min.

12

Material-oriented visualisation

In this exercise we want to tell a story with everyday objects. The next time you visit a café, bar, or restaurant with friends, use the beer mat, the sugar shaker, the glass, your cutlery, and the edge of the table as a reference for your story. Watch how a scenario is created from a few objects. If the pizzeria has a paper tablecloth, it's even more fun to include it with 3D folds or simple drawing. Be careful with the wine glasses!
(Analysing ▶ Visualising)

10 min.

13

Memory log (partner exercise)

With this exercise you practise how to recall experiences, to visually reproduce sensations (and to rely on yourself and others). Let a person guide you with your eyes closed through one or more rooms. The person touches you only at the elbow and hand. Do not speak. During this time, be acutely aware of your orientation, light conditions, surfaces, smells, and noises. Afterwards, take a pen and a sheet of A4 paper and note down/draw your impressions, the path you took, and what happened. It doesn't have to be comprehensible to anyone else! Then switch roles.

10 min.

14

Motor Memory, iRobot

Have you ever experienced thinking your arm is at a 90-degree angle and it isn't at all? For this exercise, take a cup with a drink in it. Pick it up, bring it to your mouth, drink from it, and put it down. Then perform the action again without a cup. Observe exactly whether you remember the fine-motor processes, the forms your hands take, and the distances the fingers have to each other and to your mouth. We all have a motor memory, which your body uses to remember processes. Still, it is difficult to perform the same process identically. In general, we don't have to. For calligraphers, this motor memory and the brio that goes with it are essential. Mimes also use it. This aspect is of the utmost relevance in physical computing.

2 min.

15

Upside down (partner exercise)

You need a hand mirror or a mirror tile (20 × 20 cm) as a tool. One person holds the mirror very still and aligned so that the other person looks at their surroundings through the mirror but does not see him- or herself. Then both of them move very slowly together through the room/space. Your inclination and height should change occasionally as you move. One person leads, the other person experiences. Sometimes the person being guided sees the floor, sometimes the ceiling. After about five minutes, switch roles.

10 min.

16

Getting into reverse

You have to learn how to run backwards. A "rear-view mirror" is your orientation aid as you walk around in the opposite direction. You slow down, visually rewind time and observe how your perception changes in a way that enriches you.

5 min.

17

Craftsmanship

Have your parents, grandparents, or one of your best friends tell you the recipe for a favourite dish and sketch in all the details. In the next step, try to cook the dish without breaking a sweat. As a precaution, have the pizza delivery number ready. (Analysing ▶ Grasping)

1–48 h.

Short exercises on the five dimensions: Take an everyday object and answer the following questions as far as you can get. This exercise is fun in a small group too. Tip: Be curious about the object's hidden potential. Please clarify in advance who owns the object and to what extent it can be taken apart or destroyed.

5 min.–1 h. each

18

Focus on the Formal-Aesthetic Dimension

Consider only the aspects of form and function. List (to yourself and out loud) the object's characteristics and your observations. What is the function of the whole object? Which component has which function? Where can something be poured in, grasped, or pressed? What happens if it changes scale dramatically? What could the object be then? What is the most exciting part of the object and why? What else can the object do? What states and forms should the object take on during use? What other forms can the object assume? When and where does it break?

19

Focus on the Formal-Aesthetic Dimension

Consider only the aspects of construction, structure, proportion, and volume. List (to yourself and out loud) the object's characteristics and your observations. What basic volumes does the object comprise? What space does the object occupy if it is inserted into the next largest basic volume (cuboid, sphere)?

Where are the lines defining its shape? What do they look like? Where are there special points? Where in nature is there a similar structure? What are the proportions of the object? Does it follow the golden ratio? Is it based on a grid or an algorithm? What void does the object describe and what does its negative form look like? What happens when you multiply, add, or combine the same elements?

20

Focus on the Material-Haptic Dimension

Take any object and answer the questions spontaneously: What materials are used (material technology)? What material quality and properties do they have? What is the "actual" quality? Is the use of material generous, sensible, economical? What do the waste products in the production process look like or how might they look? What properties does the material have (does it stretch when heated ...) and what would you call them? In what other contexts do you find this material, this surface texture? How does the material sound, what sound can you get from it? How does the material smell and what does it remind you of? What would an "opposite" material be and what would change if the object were made of this material? Are there any analogies?

21

Focus on the Productive Dimension

This question may require some research, but it is always worth it: How do you imagine the object was produced? Can you identify and sketch out the production process and possibly abstract it visually or in terms of content?

22

Focus on the Cultural Dimension

Pick up another object within easy reach and answer the following questions for yourself: Where do we generally find this object? What does the object stand for in your culture? What would change if it were used at the North Pole, in the sauna, or in the garden? What other objects are related to it? What other objects could it be easily combined with?

23

Focus on the Interactive Dimension

Consider only the aspects of human-machine interaction, analogue and digital, and the surface of the material. List (to yourself and out loud) the object's characteristics and your observations. What surfaces are used? Where does it reflect light? What character should the surface texture impart? Where and how is the object touched? How does it feel? What interaction does the object have with the environment? (digital, analogue, mechanical; points of support, feedback ...)

24

Synaesthetise!

Close your eyes. Turn around once, open your eyes again, and fix the first object that catches your eye. Describe it and pay attention to haptics, sounds, colour and form, temperature, and everything else you perceive. What do you like about it, what not, and why? What does the object remind you of? Are there people, places, situations that you associate with it? Then the principle of synaesthesia kicks in. We find ourselves in situations that remind us of other things, places, and people or trigger special feelings. We use this in many projects. Creatives are pre-destined to be synaesthetes. (Analysing)

5 min.

25

Change of mode

In this exercise you will work with the principle of "changing mode". Over a period of three hours, you systematically alter your working mode in 30-minute cycles, focusing the whole time on one project if possible. A timer is highly recommended for this. For example, you work 30 minutes in the workshop, you draw for 30 minutes, in the next 30 minutes you take a break to think about your project, then you describe your project for 30 minutes. Now build a paper protoype and in the last step work another 30 minutes on your computer.

3 h.

26

Social root network

Think of the people closest to you for this exercise. Where do you come from and what kind of stages have you gone through in your life so far? Create a kind of map. This can be a drawing, twentieth-century style, a kind of mind map or cultural map on which you cluster and illustrate ideas in words. Describe moments visually and with short notes, identifying formal similarities, cultural or geographical factors, overlapping content. Perhaps also points of intersection where your paths have crossed.

50 min. +

27

Writing, language, fun

This exercise is about translation competence. It is best to work with at least two people. Put a beautiful object in front of you or in the middle of the group. Use a pencil and paper to write down your thoughts and a concrete description of what you see for 3 minutes in a fictitious language of your own, e.g. with the help of sign systems, hieroglyphics, or fantasy writing. And that's not all. Read your notes out loud to yourself, or even better to the other(s). (Experimenting ▶ Combining and Trying Out)

15 min.

28

Window on the Truth

Choose a photograph or an illustration on which several actions are taking place simultaneously – in A4 format, for example. Create a flexible passe-partout by cutting out two L-shaped paper surfaces. Frame the particular action and observe how the statement / level of meaning detaches itself from the context and tells a new story. This is similar to quotations where the second part of a sentence is missing. In media reporting, we don't know the full context and what else was happening in the vicinity. You can use this to create your pictures. The standard expression related to anything unwanted that is on the film: "We'll fix it in post" (i.e. in post-production).

45 min.

29

Process study

Sit down, observe, and learn. Focus for ten minutes and make a record of all the processes you observe. Create a table with the following columns: time, actor, activity/process. Your notes could look like this:
Garden, 7.45 am, bird, flies to tree / Garden, 7.45 am squirrel reacts to bird, pauses, and turns around / Pavement, 7.46 am, two passers-by cross the street / Staircase, 7.48 am, neighbour, climbs stairs. And so on. You get a feeling for the diversity and difference of processes and their possible interactions. Let the simultaneity surprise you.

10 min.

30

Genius loci walk

Go to a new or familiar place. It can be your home too. Turn on all your sensory receptors and switch off your mobile devices. Walk quietly through interiors, exteriors, and the surrounding area. With your senses now sharpened, try to capture the spirit of the place. What makes this place special? Is the building detached or semi-detached? In what direction is it oriented? What effect does the clinker façade have, or the river? Is it on a slope? Is it constantly raining, are there special sounds, or is it all bundled together? Write down your thoughts in drawings or words. Try to reduce your impressions to the essential characteristics and abstract them. The question of what seems relevant (only) at the moment and what has a lasting or recurring influence on this place can help you. Observe how a unique image is formed that describes the singularity of this place.

30 min.

31

Dynamic adaptive systems (group ≥10)

All the things in our environment are related to each other and influence or interact with one another. We transfer chaos research and system theory (cybernetics) into an applied exercise. Our algorithm: Each person chooses (secretly/mentally) two people from the group and tries to position him- or herself between them. Since these two people are also actively involved, all the positions change adaptively. There are no static states.

5 min.

32

Measure me

Measure your body precisely in both static and dynamic states, i.e. taking large steps, small steps, goose-stepping, and standing. You determine the following measurements: heights (e.g. eye level), lengths (e.g. foot, stride length) as well as distances between the legs (e.g. span of thumb and index finger, arm span). Determine at least one dimension with your hand and one with your step that you can call up exactly and easily at any time. You will see how well you measure the next time you buy a shelf with spread fingers without a folding ruler, or how you calculate the size of the rooms when viewing a flat.

30 min.

33

Chance ingredient

Have you ever sprinkled figures with coffee powder or mixed your acrylic colours with curry? Go to the kitchen and choose the food powders and liquids that have potential to contribute to an interesting working method or colour mixture. Paint with wine or oil. Combine familiar representational tools, like a charcoal pencil, with unfamiliar ones like shaving foam! You can create new structures and new colours. Take advantage of the "accidental" sense of liberation that removes any residual fears of the blank piece of paper. (Experimenting ▶ Combining and Trying Out)

15 min.

34

Perfect taste

If you love cooking or are in the mood for it, use it to model the creative process of implementation. When do you decide what will end up on your plate? Are you more the "cookbook" type or the "whatever's in the fridge" type (if there's anything in it at all)? Implementing while you're cooking means: composing, cooking, finishing, seasoning, tasting. (Realising ▶ Completing)

1–24 h.

35

The it-thing

Choose any item from a current situation and present it to colleagues, your family, or yourself in front of a mirror. You have three minutes to convince your audience that the object is THE thing. What is the nature of the object? Is it particularly valuable, well designed, badly designed, etc.? Turn everyday characteristics into something special, give them charisma. (Realising ▶ Presenting)

15 min.

36

From documentation to inspiration

In our last exercise, I suggest you start a personal long-term project: the sketchbook. It is a collection of thoughts and drawings that anyone actively involved in design should cultivate. From now on you have it with you wherever you go, and it helps you to document (on a regular basis) your own work, ideas, and sources of inspiration in the form of sketches (on unlined paper) and to develop them further. It can also become the place for any important notes you take on the project, somewhere where all kinds of things can be bundled together more quickly. (Realising ▶ Documenting)

∞

I have so many designs and video ideas in my head, so I always try to be productive.
— BILLIE EILISH

How can I try out the method?

For projects at the university I usually determine the manufacturing process or the material, rather than specifying the result. Because in the method you come up with your very own project ideas, the path is the goal. Here are a few approaches you can follow to develop your practice:

▶ a room structure (max. 1 m²) made of cardboard or paper

▶ an object using a casting technique

▶ a 3D object using fabric

▶ an installation using string

▶ a spatial structure using light

▶ a logo for a sustainable fashion label

▶ a moving object that can double its size

▶ a sole for a new running shoe

Tips on organising your work

If you have decided to carry out your project with someone else or in a group, then I have the following recommendations. You will increase the likelihood of a constructive and productive cooperation. The tips range from basic to pro and should include something for everyone.

▶ Maybe you work effectively with your best friends, although that's not something you can take for granted. Discuss the worst-case scenario and an exit strategy in advance if the collaboration does not work in the long run. Sometimes it fails because of money issues. Get clear on this up front. The friendship should not be damaged. In any case, you will train your soft skills in teamwork. Perhaps your colleagues will become friends or have become friends. Successfully carrying out projects together strengthens trust. The probability that someone will come back to you increases with each of these projects. How to deal constructively with defeats/ setbacks is another aspect of it. Friction is inevitable, just like in real life. The circle of people with whom you cooperate consistently and well could also form the basis for a joint enterprise.

▶ You probably know how to set up your own structure for working in. A laptop, electricity, and a telephone and internet connection, a chair and a table—sometimes that's all you need. In addition to healthy food and a restful place to sleep. Depending on the nature of your new project, you will be out and about collecting information, talking to people, or busy in your kitchen with all kinds of exciting materials.

▶ Before you start, talk briefly about what you expect from the joint project. From the project itself and from the other people involved. Are there any ideas about this and if so, who imagines what and in what way? You can also use these questions to become aware of your strengths. What do you contribute in particular? What are you good at? What would you like to familiarise yourself with? It may well be that in certain phases the work is shared in a professional way and yet you still learn from each other. If you need help, step in for each other, to the extent that it is technically and functionally possible.

▶ At the start and before taking any important steps in the process, compare your quality standards. How detailed do you want to get? What level of imprecision will you put up with? What purpose should this step serve?

▶ Be patient with each other, personally and professionally. Give others time to complete the particular step in the work.[88]

▶ Under what conditions will your cooperation take place?

▶ Create temporal and infrastructural space for sharing. Are you meeting at your current (shared) workplace after hours, in your own home, or at the university, or do you get together in cafés or coworking spaces or a mix of everything? Your experiments may need a place where you have some authority and control. Oscillate between a chaotic desk that stimulates the brain and a clean workplace, especially when working with materials and tools. Clarify which media you prefer and what kind of communication culture you want to develop and maintain together.

▶ It is relatively rare to work together exclusively in analogue form on-site. Clarify which digital platforms you want to use to exchange information. For security reasons, it can be

Important key qualifications for designers

Methodological competence

What you use to find various ways from A to B. Expertise in process development, creative know-how, problem-solving competence, developing meaningful solution strategies, ability to analyse, transfer/transmit, research/procure information, time management ...

Individual competence

How you act, your personality structure, creativity, self-confidence, self-motivation, initiative, pleasure in your own process of development, flexibility, sense of responsibility, reliability ...

Design competence

Ability to act as a designer. Key qualifications of designers: soft skills, hard skills, social skills.

Social competence

How you function/act in a team and with other people, ability to work in a team, tolerance, ability to communicate, ability to cooperate, ability to criticise, ability to deal with conflict ...

hard skills

soft skills

social skills

important to determine the server location. Create a project account on your own server or with international providers such as Slack, Dropbox, or Google docs. In Germany, for example, you can store 2–30 GB free of charge on German server locations at Deutsche Post, Deutsche Telekom, web.de, and gmx.de. Git Hub is ideal for open source developments. With notion.so you have a free all-in-one workspace for professional project organisation. Figma.com is helpful and free of charge for up to three projects around working together on digital products. With whimsical.com or miro.com you can create up to four digital shared mind maps or sticky notes free of charge.

▶ Regular personal meetings to exchange ideas and information are essential.

▶ For a complex issue, you can seek out experts together or report back afterwards.

▶ This is not a contradiction, but a professional approach: identify yourself with your actions, but keep your ego in check. It's about making common cause. If the other person has a different (cultural or professional) background, interdisciplinarity can be very enriching! Perhaps you can incorporate this specific knowledge into your project. And, above all, treat each other's ideas with respect. Create shared experiences.

▶ On timing: mostly time gets budgeted automatically "to save time"! Time management creates structure. Think beforehand how much time you give yourself for a step, an experiment, or a piece of research. Perhaps you plan it as a short-term project, in which you can work intensively to obtain (and test) a result in a relatively short space of time. In service design^G, design sprints with brief successive intervals are common. In design thinking, microtiming is used, in which only a few minutes are available for particular work steps. Think before your next step how much time you want to give it and how flexible you want to be about the time factor. An hour, a (working) day or as long as it takes. Then, in between, you can change the mode (→ 81). If necessary, arrange fixed times for communication and non-communication.

▶ Have the willingness and openness to familiarise yourself with each new project. Learning takes time. Thanks to our expertise as translators, we designers come into contact with a wide variety of thematic areas. We analyse work processes in companies in order to design an interior space, we prepare scientific content for exhibitions, or devise cool new marketing campaigns. With each project, we not only gain experience but also become a little bit smarter. Designers are always passionate about what they do. We have our fingers on the pulse, looking ahead. We formulate solutions and visions and encourage people to engage with current events. We jump nimbly between traditional techniques and avant-garde approaches, our senses attuned to our materials and their qualities. We acquire new tools and programs in order to juggle with them and explore limits. Lifelong learning is the job profile. Working professionally in a creative context is both a career and a mission. That's the beauty of the job!

But I'm pretty good with collaborative thinking. I work well with other people.
– DAVID BOWIE

Tips on 3D visualising

**Databases are the new
semi-finished products.
Designers as toolmakers.**

It is important that in every project we can find a means of expression with which we are able to communicate in an adequate and time-efficient way. Depending on the stage of the project, the medium is different. So sometimes a mock-up, a dummy, a model, or a 1:1 detail is the right step to take to become clearer in the design and to communicate with others. Spatial objects, prototypes and models are ultimately three-dimensional visualisations, regardless of whether they are created in digital or analogue form. Fusion360 is a good free program for 3D modelling. SketchUp.com with the model library 3D Warehouse enables you to create 3D visualisations easily and without prior knowledge of modelling. Or draw simple diagrams free of charge with draw.io. Databases for CAD and 3D printing models include Grab CAD and Thingiverse as well as the search engine for 3D printable models yeggi.com. With SnazzyMaps you can customise the shape, colour, and style of Google Maps. Thenounproject offers thousands of icons. This trend was once pioneered by stock photography, along with FontShop. You will find numerous tutorials on the web. Models communicate our idea in different degrees of perfection and detail (low or high fidelity) and materials. Sometimes we use physical objects or artefacts in advanced stages of our projects to test functionality or other people's perceptions of what we are seeking to do. Models, artefacts, and prototypes literally enable others to understand our idea.

In 3D modelling, input is currently done through 3D scans or digital engineering drawings created with trackpads, keyboards, drawing pads, and mouses. But why can't it also be voice controlled for everyone or done with the help of a simple gesture? One sweeping hand movement and the file is already in the computer. Back in 1939 at the World's Fair, the robot and his dog, Elektro and Sparko, listened to voice commands. Voice control as an input format is almost a commonplace, while intuitive gestures and movements in interaction still leave room for improvement. To generate data models, we can also fall back on construction plans and instructions, the collective knowledge from the net. Every day, new services and platforms are springing up to cater to the creation of objects. Scanning, modelling, producing, customising, recycling. Databases are the new semi-finished products. New technologies, digital tools, affordable production equipment – such as the 3D printer and the infrastructure that is being developed with it (fab lab, for example) – support local production possibilities with dynamic potential. Design, development, and production are merging, and communication designers, like product designers, are increasingly becoming production designers and toolmakers. Logo makers like tailorbrands.com will do the work for most companies.

A brief look at the future prospects suggests that designers will work more on system developments, operating from completely different locations. Design agencies are becoming more and more part of management consultancies such as Accenture and McKinsey, who have done a survey to quantify the value of design for market-oriented companies.[89]

Methods

Methods provide stability. For designers, researchers, or children. Something is created step-by-step in a way that is comprehensible and can ideally be measured as it passes through the different steps. A method helps to increase the probability that what is desired will happen. Methods do not guarantee maximum results. They can show us a way, but they shouldn't make us think less. We have to think for ourselves.

When we write a quote, divided up into job items based on different performance phases, we think our way structurally through the project. This is a first methodical step in the design process. Let us be guided methodically (e. g. by the five dimensions) but never forget to trust our intuition.

We should always be able to argue for and defend our creative decisions. It is perfectly legitimate to make a decision intuitively and then figure out the arguments. Heuristics deals with how we solve problems unconventionally, quickly, and relatively unerringly. Our individual stock of experience has a significant impact on the decisions we make.

Emotional and spontaneous factors like our intuition are on an equal footing with these analytical procedures. Our gut feeling is trained and strengthened by experience. Researchers have found that intuitive decisions can be very accurate, regardless of memory load and the number of mental tasks being managed in parallel. According to their studies, rational decisions tended to be conservative.[90]

We can use this method to charge our store of intuition. In his brilliant article "Intuition Is the Key to Good Design", interface designer Professor Boris Müller, a dear colleague of mine, argues that we can recharge and even teach intuition.[91]

Intuition is the sister of perception. Just as perception generates inspiration when it falls on fertile ground, intuition is the act of drawing on our wealth of experience when making decisions. Then we can use our previous knowledge to double-check. First belly, then head. If there are too many things going against the decision, we rethink it.

Let us also trust in our common sense and ask: How can I move the project on? I applied the principle of the Cultural probe in my diploma thesis. That was in 1997. The reference books say that this method was invented in 1999. Sometimes we make methodical steps out of the logical requirements of the project without using a method explicitly established for this purpose. We should have faith in ourselves!

Schematic representations of methodological sequences simplify the complexity, so that in general the operational sequence can be clearly communicated. The model of the method with the five dimensions, as you have learned it so far (→ 12, 14, 30, and 62), is chronologically oriented, with a constant, linear progression of time imputed to the project. We seldom experience creative processes as linear. The creative loop is presented on page 37 as a diagram. If method diagrams show possible processes or content as a network or web, completely different images can arise. The principles of order can be spatial, energetic, temporal, content-related, or structural. In his final thesis at the FH Potsdam, Jens Rauenbusch observed in his analysis of visual representations of design thinking and design processes that the visual presentations of processes rarely correspond to the real dynamics of the processes.

Method or not, it is important to realise that the creative process is sometimes uncomfortable (for us) and we have to endure it in order to move forward. Without effort, special things seldom happen!

Intuition is the sister of perception.

Design team culture
Peter Merholz and Kristin Skinner, *Org Design for Design Orgs: Building and Managing In-House Design Teams* (Sebastopol, CA: O'Reilly Media, 2016)

Recommendations for further study:

Design thinking
Robert Gerlach: threebility.com
Martin Tomitsch et al., *Design. Think. Make. Break. Repeat: A Handbook of Methods* (Amsterdam: BIS, 2018)
Dark Horse Innovation, *Digital Innovation Playbook* (Hamburg: Murmann, 2019)

Materials
Daniel Kula and Élodie Ternaux, *Materiology: The Creative Industry's Guide to Materials and Technologies* (Basel: Birkhäuser, 2013)

Philosophy and spaces
Gaston Bachelard, *The Poetics of Space* (New York: Penguin, 2014)

Intuition
Malcolm Gladwell, *Blink: The Power of Thinking without Thinking* (London: Penguin, 2006)

Design research
Simon Grand and Wolfgang Jonas (Eds.), *Mapping Design Research* (Basel: Birkhäuser, 2012)

In part C you will find suggestions and guidelines on how to deal with a material, the dimensions of space and time, and what approaches you could follow for your project. This section of the book with its plethora of pictures is a potential source of inspiration for you in the process. Just dip into it when you're in between things.

Inspiring experiment

Principles for creating with method

This section of the book is designed to complement the description of method, offering a way to hone your vision even more and awakening your appetite for trying things out. On the following pages you will find eighty-four principles for dealing with space, time, light, colour, structure, and material as a starter pack for your project. You will find a collection of materials from realised studies, experiments, and projects that can serve as a source of inspiration in the creative process, in terms of both method and theme. Here you are welcome to browse the experimental phase and move your project forward with new ideas you've taken on board.

The principles are explained briefly using specific examples. They are all derived from exercises, studies, and projects that were developed by students I supervised using the 5D method. You will also see the results of short exercises in which the five dimensions serve as the sole starting point, without prior analysis of a work of art. You will also find an example of how the method can be used in an ongoing project. Go your own way and develop new working approaches. Let yourself be surprised by the potential of the everyday things around you.

Some projects and experiments are rounded out with keywords from the matrix, marked with an ↓. They were crucial in the development of the project. They are meant to serve you as both orientation and inspiration and indicate the interpretative bandwidth of your keywords.

$$42$$
$$+42$$
$$\overline{84}$$

"My creativity always seemed inexhaustible to me, but the flow of ideas sometimes comes to a standstill. The methodology helps find new sources of inspiration and gets the process moving again."

—MAIKE PANZ
PRODUCT DESIGNER

Space
Time
Light
Colours
Structure
Material

Space

Space starts whenever we shift beyond two dimensions. Physical space has the three dimensions of length, breadth, and height expressed as x, y, and z coordinates. If we go a little further into this topic, we soon arrive at string theories, space-time and hyperspace, but that's not where we're heading. Please regard the concept of space here as a mental construct that primarily describes architectural physical space and includes social, digital, and spatial interaction.

In this chapter, you will find examples of how you can use space creatively, how you can relate objects and knowledge in three dimensions and include them in your design. Projects and studies show you how to identify, measure, abstract, and scale positive and negative volumes, how to experiment with spatial perception, investigate the three-dimensionality of matter, use a structural principle as a study for interspaces, or digitally manipulate spatial axes, document and stage the sound and choreography of movements through space, and design interfaces to digital space with poetic/sensual gestures.

The chapter also contains an example of how to access other people's/users' conceptual space and knowledge. It shows you how to participatively enhance your level of knowledge. Another example illustrates how the method can be used in a project that is already up and running.

Our heads are round so our thoughts can change direction.
— FRANCIS PICABIA

In the other chapters you will find additional suggestions:

Immersive experience
Light / Outer space → 155

Public space
Light / Warm night → 170

Space and time
Time / Curtain → 138

Gravity
Colour / Aquarium → 176

Centrifugal forces
Light / X-ray → 166

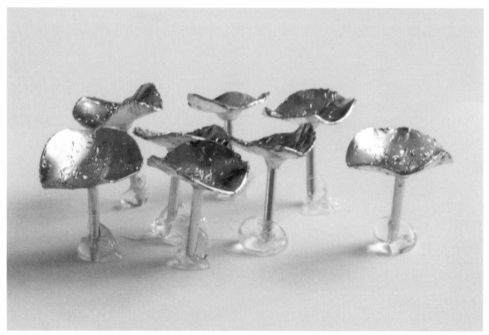

1st
principle

Changing the spatial relationship
Small things are not so small when they are put in relation to even smaller things. Everything is relative. The umbrella shape of a drawing pin is transformed into a floral shape with minimal mechanical effort and becomes a forest or an item of décor for a (relatively small) room.

2nd
principle

Developing a tool for form finding
This model is made with acrylic glass and cotton buds. A movable net structure serves as a modular principle for form finding. The shafts are connected with cords on the surface. Pulling the cords changes the shape of the model, creating variant forms.

Idea: A ceiling element and its changing movements might relate to the volume of the place. The room interacts with the user.

Mini tip: Take a look in the kitchen or bathroom before you buy expensive model-making materials.

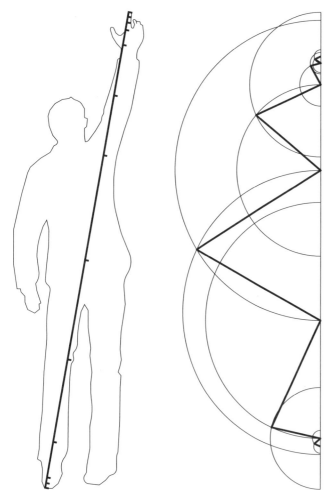

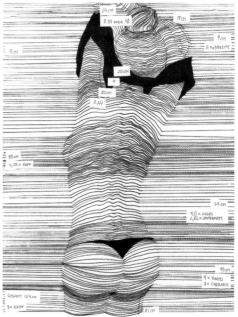

Twelve measures define
the distance between
eleven joints. Made as a
preliminary study for an
object in which proportions
are an essential design
feature.

3rd
principle

**The human form as a basis
for measuring proportions**

The golden ratio has shaped Western
culture. The proportions of the
Modulor by architect Le Corbusier
is based on the golden mean.
Orientation points that you take from

the measurements of your own body
are automatically related to each
other. A layout is the distribution and
composition of elements on a plane.
Find a use for them in a layout, poster
design, pattern, or grid.

→ Visualising your own body
measurements can lead you to
reconfigure a surface or a volume.
Mini tip: The white areas in the
layout are like the rests in a piece of
music.

*Fashion is
architecture:
it is a matter of
proportions.*
— COCO CHANEL

4th
principle

**Space in the picture, dissolving
form through transparency**
A person moves at different speeds,
in a choreography of movements
under a thin transparent membrane,
dancing with a material. The air
circulation creates unusual shapes.

→ The human body is usually quickly
recognised. You can create dynamic
tension by gently distorting it …

5th
principle

Use abstraction to give scope for interpretation

The plastic on a twist tie is compressed along the wire. Joining several of them together creates an organic structure. Placing them in the right context gives them meaning. The volume is adequately defined by the projecting branches of the tree model and the shadows they cast, creating a comprehensible form. You don't have to see all the leaves.

→ White objects have a high degree of abstraction (aesthetic value) and give the viewer the maximum scope for interpretation.

Mini tip: Make your scale model unique with unobtrusive details that are full of character.

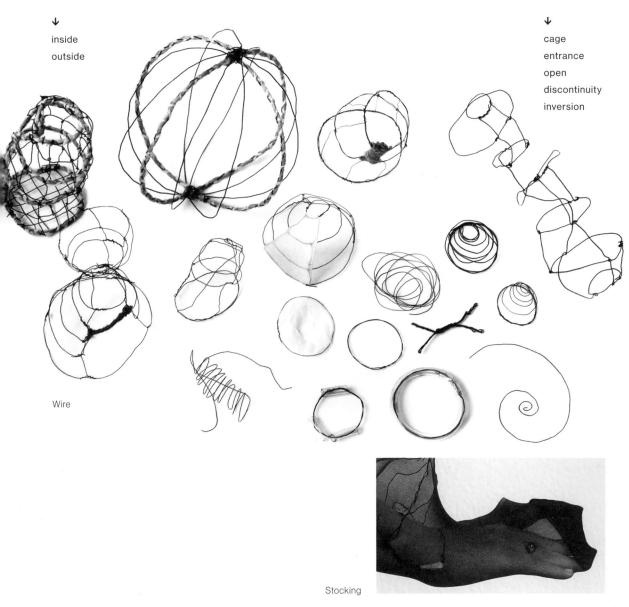

↓
inside
outside

↓
cage
entrance
open
discontinuity
inversion

Wire

Stocking

6th
principle

**Abstraction through spatial
and line-based sketches**
When does a solid appear open or
closed? Do surfaces need to be
closed to define a space? In (3D)
modelling, space is created by lines
and curves (splines) that run along
nodes.

The study with wire, string, and paper
is examining how much "inside" it
takes to get an "outside" (a combination of the Formal-Aesthetic and
Material-Haptic Dimensions). The
scope is to develop a physical shell.
Developing a study for a 3D extension
of the arm using a stocking and wire
to abstract the shape of the hand.

→ If you are devising a pictogram[G]
or infographic, ask yourself: What are
the essential formal lines that guide
perception? What is the minimum
amount of information I want to give
the user, and how much imagination
do they have to use in addition?
Working with wire can also be helpful
here.

7th
principle

Let the manufacturing process tell its story

Study of negative space: Plaster of Paris is poured into a woolly hat. Once the plaster goes hard, the hat is removed. Fibre residues remain in the plaster, with the knitting pattern determining the surface structure. The positioning of the hat during the curing period defines the shape.

→ Think of any necessary seams, joins, or traces on the surface as design elements with potential. Make profitable use of the surface texture of a body in your design work.

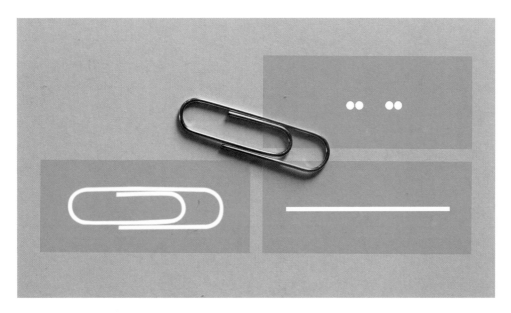

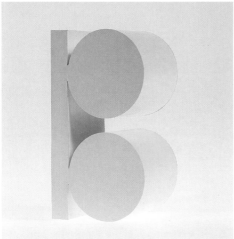
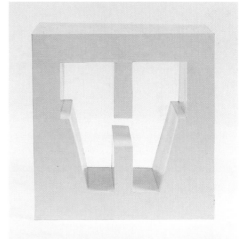

8th

principle

Spatial description

We rarely look at the actual volume of the things that surround us from all the different sides. Most of the time we are less aware of the mass than the outer surface.

A starting point for designing a font is the volume study of a paperclip; the different spatial demands are striking. The paper clip is flat because it is used between pieces of paper.

In the letter B the counters are included in the design of a letter made of paper. The W is only defined by the surrounding space that materialises.

→ Take a look at the cross section.

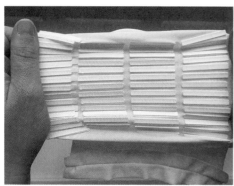

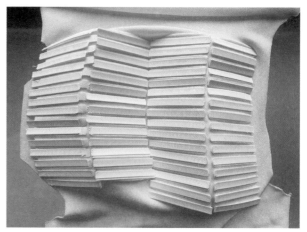

9th

principle

Pop-up, dynamic flat-pack

Study of smart textiles: A simple graphic pattern is printed with PLA (polylactic acid) in a fine 3D layer onto a stretched nylon fabric. The fabric is pulled in opposite directions on the printing plate and fixed. The warm plastic settles into the fine mesh when it is pressed. Once the printing process is complete and the fabric has been removed from the press, the surface springs up into three dimensions as the fabric pulls back into its original shape. You can stretch elastic fabrics as you print them and thus make intelligent use of tensile and compressive forces.

→ Producing something flat and then expanding it into three dimensions also works wonderfully as a classic paper pop-up.

10th
principle

**Interspaces; assembly
with a plug-in principle**
When you create interiors and
exteriors, you create exciting
interspaces.
Study of the representation of a
cloud: Equal-sized plastic panels

are slit at the ends and inserted into
each other. Two panels are enough to
create a three-dimensional space.
→ If you develop architectural
spaces and sequences of rooms on
different levels, the plug-in principle
is a quick solution to support your

spatial imagination in the design
process. Combining this principle
with diagonals and angles is complex
and generates intriguing insights.

Space   ↓

playful

sonorous

emotional

mysterious

ephemeral

interactive

11th
principle

Mindsets for the visitor: The pre-set
Project on physical perception with a challenging round of sensory impressions, like sound and touch in a black room. Visitors are stimulated by questions beforehand. Visitors find messages like "Try smelling with your shoulder" before and during their walk through the room.
→ Create the mindset you want your visitor to take away with them! Have them see things through your eyes!

12th
principle

User testing, feedback, evaluation: The post-set
In the same project, visitors are asked about the quality of their spatial experience after going through the room. It is important for the project group to find out what is going on in the people and to conduct interviews with the visitors. There are spaces that do not work, but they keep being built because nobody checks the practical usage. A shower makes no sense in a particular spot or a door does not open. Socio-spatial user studies test completed buildings and rooms when they are being lived in to derive lessons for future buildings. Do your own studies in which your room/object/process is tested and you will be able to do even better next time. High visitor numbers in an exhibition can be an indication of a good exhibition—or of a successful social media campaign. If you're wondering whether your spatial installation really works, then do the evaluation. Observe the users and ask them questions. Feedback is a gift!

13th
principle

The poetry of gesture in interaction

How do we want to operate devices and obtain services in the future? Keyboards will soon be history and voice input can't be the whole story. Intuitive gestures and spatial movement are a wide-open field — and it will be fun for all of us.

→ In your project, consciously use the sensuality of a gesture in the interaction with an object or space, both digital and analogue.

14th
principle

Returning to the archetype

Study: The input comes via the laptop camera, which recognises the high-contrast markings of a pen tip. The distance and position of the nib determine the output and what appears on the monitor. The whole process is controlled by Wekinator, a free open-source program for interacting with self-learning machines, which has been developed for controlling drums. It is very easy to operate since it works without programming. The image on the monitor is dynamically changed by a tool from Processing, an open-source programming language.

Context: Questioning the purpose and ergonomics of processes and tools at the digital analogue interface. Transfer the use of an object into a new context.

→ When you design (digital) interaction in space, you determine how intuitive the movement or gesture can be and what tools you make available. Ask yourself whether there is an archetype of the movement or process. Is it the finger writing in the sand or is there an intermediate stage as there is with the pen?

Space

 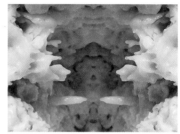

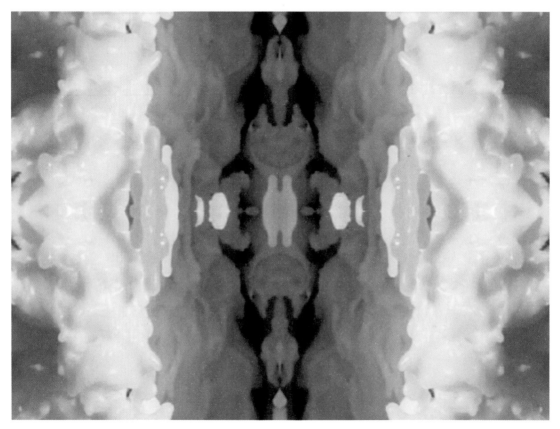

15th
principle

Recomposing the space in the image

The reflection of a room in the image, mirrored along the vertical and horizontal axes, recomposes the space. We identify reflections in the vertical much faster than in the horizontal. The aim of the study is to create a spatial experience and to give wax, which is a warm material, a cool appearance. The process of altering the space is recorded in a video. Modifications in the colour tone and the sound (hollow, dripping, clangorous, technical) create a surreal space in the picture. This video is projected on all four walls of a space and played back in a loop choreographed in time. The presentation in a closed space underlines the intensity.

→ Work at the interface of image and space by getting away from our familiar (Euclidean) ways of looking at things and natural laws such as gravitational force.

↓
dissolving the space
endless

*Physical contact is
a human necessity.*
– DAVID BYRNE

16th
principle

Mock-up, dummy, prototyping
Study of a spatial installation in which the breath can be experienced in three dimensions as you walk through it. The parameters – the movement of the space itself (wall and ceiling), its materiality (plastic sheeting), sound, and coloured light – are intended to express fragility and physical balance.

→ For analogue spatial experiences, build a simple simulation at a scale of 1:1 to see the effect in advance and test it out.

Space

↓
perspective
shadow
spatial drawing
layered
stage-like

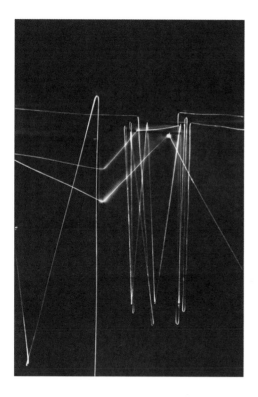

17th
principle

Manipulating and designing spatial orientation
In a series of dark rooms, light is discreetly fed into an acrylic cord and traverses the space. The intention is to investigate the object-(subject)-line-space-motion relationships.
→ When the room becomes a stage.

Confuse visitors with restrictions and the removal of any perpendiculars, and guide them through the space with your choreography.

Mini silent-film tip for studying
stagecraft and perspective:
The Cabinet of Dr. Caligari.
Old as the hills (1920) but a must.

18th
principle

**Using the fun factor:
Physical interaction**
The product, which the viewer
generates in the form of tone,
volume, and speed, controls the
movement of an interactive ceiling
element. It reacts to sound by means
of a sensor, an Arduino board, and
pulleys. It is not the direct body
movement that is captured, as

with a Kinect camera – rather the
focus is on the creativity involved in
generating the sounds.
Project context/task: Development
of a 3D structure. The interactive
dimension plays an important role in
developing the project. Mechanics,
editing, and technology are optimised
for the movement sequences.

→ Most people love surprises.
Reward curiosity. Play with the
unforeseen. Have other people
discover something new.

19th

principle

Transferability as common denominator: Use substructure

The context of the project is the design of a campaign to raise awareness for Amnesty International. The Cultural Dimension is the kernel and starting point of the project, which aims to give the public an understanding of Amnesty International's commitment to human rights. The guerrilla campaign concept involves using monuments as witnesses to previous actions. The smallest form of monument, street signposting, is chosen because it is easy to implement and makes use of existing substructures. One of the great potentials of the project is its global transferability because in every city there are streets named after important people and events.

→ The simplest things can also be the most effective. Think about how and whether your project could be implemented in other places with simple means and what would be needed for it. This will also move you forward in your own project.

20th
principle

The interactive social space as an extension of your own perception: Mapping
Context: Developing a map of favourite places in Berlin's Moabit

district. The local neighbourhood is involved as part of a public event. People mark their favourite shop on a map, so that the map is constantly growing.

→ Mapping is an exciting procedure for getting to know people, habits, and places and understanding a place layer by layer. Try it out for yourself. Don't be afraid of people.

All communication relies on the
goodwill of the other.

—MAX FRISCH

Study of the role/responsibility of
the individual in public space. A
competition in which teams collect
rubbish over a certain period and are
measured on an improvised rubbish

scale is intended to sensitise park
visitors to the issue of littering and
the maintenance of green spaces.

→ Communicating with the target
group. Develop a format in which
you can enter into a dialogue in an
experimental or result-oriented way.
Inform others and get informed!

Space

Inhabited space
transcends
geometrical space.
– GASTON BACHELARD

21st
principle

Role play to test spatial sequences
This is a sample project for applying the method (without analysis of an artistic work) in a programme that is already up and running.
Context: The development of a floor plan for a student residence with a focus on sustainability, based on the premise that sharing is prior to owning. The Interactive Dimension will be combined with the project context and the issue of human-human interaction question is highlighted: Does a shared seven-person flat work with small private rooms and a large community area and where are the snags in the spatial sequencing? As a proof of concept, a 1:1 floor plan is sketched, and a sample daily routine is performed as a role play

and edited on video. The bathrooms must be designed in such a way that several people can use them independently of each other at the same time. The role play is a proven method of gaining knowledge, as the participants act empathically

and can thus give constructive feedback. The 1:1 scale is always highly recommended. It only takes a few essential features to create the space and a little imagination from everyone involved.

→ Try to define individual modules in complex questions and give the method a go. Focus on a part of the problem and play through the five dimensions systematically.

Time

Are you thinking, How can I work with time in my project?
I don't have any ...?

It doesn't always take a lot of time to work with the time element in your project. Some (time-based) studies and experiments can actually be done very fast, and they don't require much, sometimes just a piece of sliced bread or a couple of screws. If you're thematising time in your project, then it might take a little longer ...

In this chapter, you will find examples of how you can tackle your project when time is a key factor. For example, you can measure time or, by the same token, you can not measure it but rather let things happen. Observing the processes might be a source of inspiration.

On the following pages, you will find suggestions for how you can work sequentially by setting individual images in motion using stop-motion technology, how you can follow the course of an event or support growth and processes of change (material/mould → **224**), how you can observe and document, how you can poetically record an ephemeral material, how you can create a sense of dynamic tension by compressing and stretching time periods in a video animation, or how you can create data in real time as abstract visualisation. Of course, time is also connected to space and everything we do, which is why it's so intriguing. The sound that may feature in videos and films is also there in the space. So everything is connected.

In the other chapters you will find additional food for thought:

Movement in space

Concurrent courses of action

Time exposure

Time   ↓

variable

shadow

urban

3D

typographic

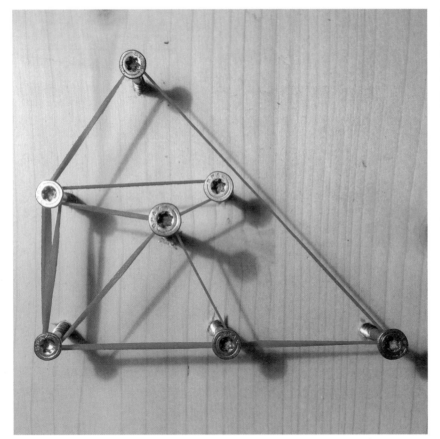

22nd
principle

**Using traces of the process
as a design resource**
A wooden board bears witness to
a moment in time. The holes are
the traces of old configurations.
Using a lace and screws inserted
in a board, you can create lines in
space. If you adjust the screws to
different heights, the 3D aspect is
accentuated, especially the shadows
that are thrown.

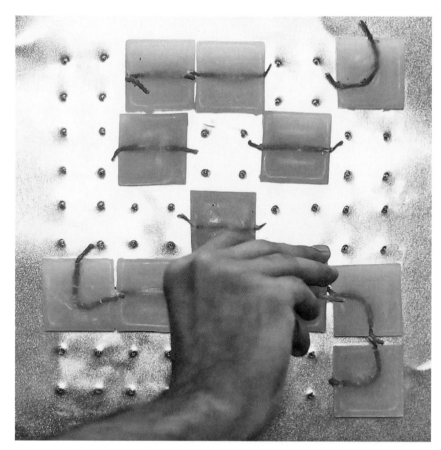

↓
modular
changing direction

  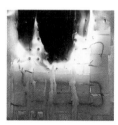

23rd
principle

Tension through inexorability

Context: Modularity and change of direction should become the functional design elements of an object. A music video shows two hands putting wax cubes on a vertical panel. The red wick runs through the middle of each cube as connection. When the surface is full, they burn one after the other. Some of the wicks are "disrupters" and are misaligned. Shortly before the candle threatens to go out, the wax cube is exchanged. In the video, the length of time the wicks burn is tailored to the music, compressed and stretched so that a "drama" arises around the question: Will the flame go out? – All's well that ends well.

→ Release your inner drama queen and use it in the time layer of your design!

24th
principle

**An animated character by
way of an object study**
Context: While exploring the
potential of a chip fork, the student
stumbles on representational
objects, produced as the fork is

heated and melts. Drawings showing
the deformation of the fork are
transformed into a stop-motion film
in which the viewer finally disappears
into the large gullet of the fork.

→ Inspiration for an animated
character lurks in the smallest
everyday objects. Let yourself be
inspired by a material and transfer
the qualities and behaviour to
drawings. In a flipbook, perhaps.

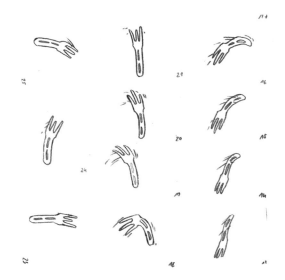

135

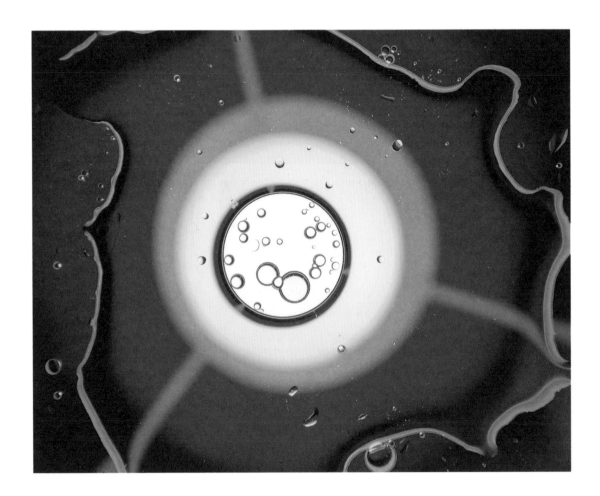

25th
principle

**Get images to dance in
time to the beat**
Studies of oil and water in which
surfaces in the image react to each
other. Oil is added drop by drop to a
bowl of water illuminated from below
and turned into a stop-motion film.
The different speeds of movement
are matched to the rhythm of the
music. The varying surface tensions
of the liquids create a multitude of
compositions. Distortions are caused

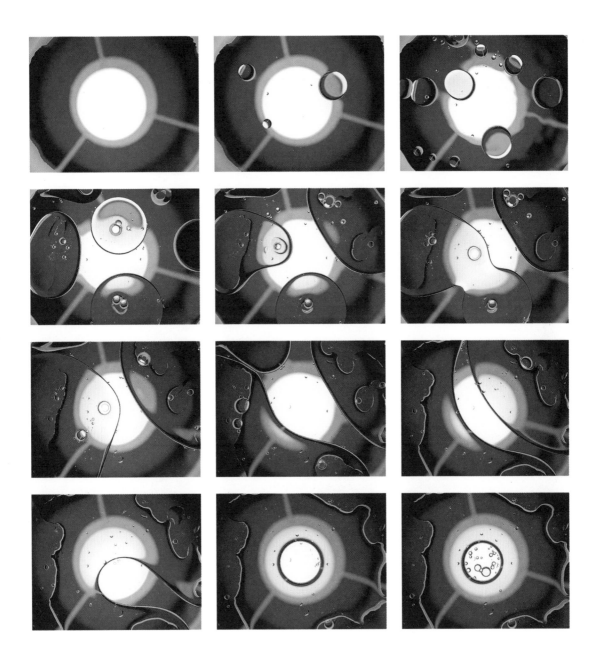

by the magnifying-glass effect.
You create tension by extending and
compressing time as you synchronise
image and sound.

→ Use music to get inspiration for
the speed of your film.

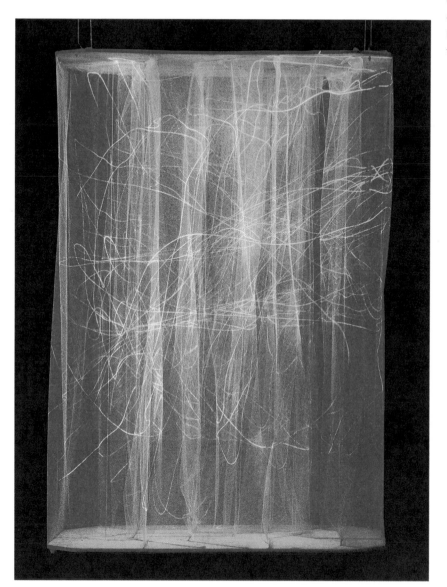

26th
principle

**Atmospheric visualisation
in real time**
Context: An abstract visualisation
of the soundscape (audio data) of
a place is projected onto a curtain.
Two places, one static and one

dynamic (train), are to be connected
in real time with the idea of digitally
fusing location and information. A
construction of chipboard and tulle
impregnated with luminous paint
provides the projection surface. The

floor and top panel are shaped like
the Ringbahn – the railway round the
centre of Berlin – which the sound
recordings are transmitted from.
Based on the technical input of the
audio data (decibels), a laser draws

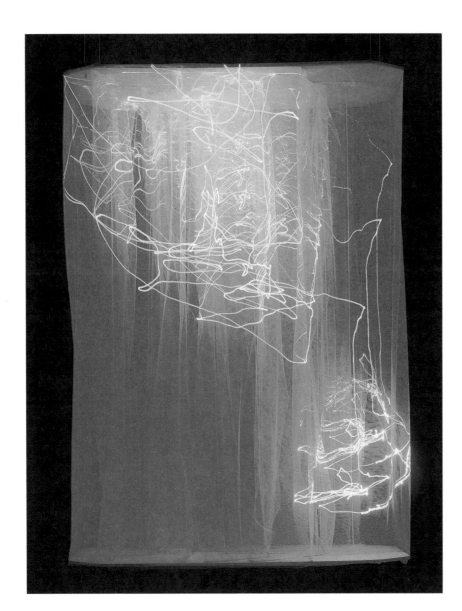

*I have to be seen
to be believed.*
—Queen Elizabeth II

a line in a loop. It changes, fades, and is redrawn. The loop refers to the train line, which also moves in a circle.

→ Where do you get facts and figures from? Do you measure quantitatively or qualitatively? Are you interested in an atmospheric picture or clear statements? In a data visualisation, you decide

how comprehensible you want the information to be. If the information content on a certain topic can be quantitatively measured, then the viewer will be able to understand the context.

Silence

27th
principle

**Experimental typography
with time-based media**

Context: The aim is a video against audism, a form of discrimination against people who are deaf or hard of hearing. The video was made together with a deaf person. A study on space and time in multi-dimensional sign language. German sign language is an independent, natural, and fully fledged language defined by hand orientation, temporal sequencing, and movement. In addition, deaf people use the finger alphabet. This is used, for example,

↓
time-based
communicative
physical
provocative
multidimensional

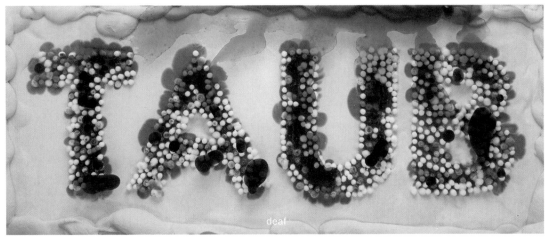

to spell names. Matches cast in plaster of Paris burn and produce the word *Höllenlärm* (pandemonium). Colour slowly impregnates cotton buds, turning them red like blood.

Letters made of blue foam are placeholders for experiments with water and ice. Letter-shaped ice melts. Cold stands for peace and quiet in the film.

→ Do you have a specific topic that interests you? Then make it the subject of your project!

Pandemonium

28th

principle

Colour changes over time
Study on time-based material change. Sliced bread is toasted a piece at a time, each slice going into the toaster for one additional minute. Some areas on the surface are moistened with water, and the toast browns more slowly here.

→ Transfer the interplay of elegant pallor and crunchy brownness into an analogue pixel graphic!

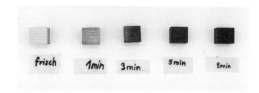

29th
principle

Intensity through time

Material studies of a wooden cube are used as a starting point for a data visualisation. As burning leads to an undefined cuboid shape, the wooden cubes are fried in a pan.

Numbers in space: The statistical values of forest fires in the German state of Brandenburg by year, area, and amount of damage are displayed three-dimensionally. The idea is to create a visual impression of fire-prone spruce monocultures arranged in rows.

The growth sizes of (threatened) seahorses, their territorial behaviour and delicate movement in the water and their habitat, which includes mangroves, sea grass, and coral reefs, inspire a mobile.

→ Use statistics, movement patterns, and temporal change processes in your research object as a source for size units.

↓
individuality
longevity
additive
graphic
colourful

Study of organic colouring agents and plant dyes that can be produced by the researchers themselves. Fresh or dried plant matter is brought to a boil. Small plaster discs are put in the water for 1 hour, 8 hours, and 24 hours. In one study, the coloured water is also stirred into gypsum, which ends up producing the most intense hues.

→ These colours are suitable for dyeing all sorts of things. Yellow tones: turmeric, carrot, coffee, leaves. Red-violet-grey tones: beetroot, mallow tea, pomegranate, red cabbage. Green tones: kiwi, spinach, parsley.

145

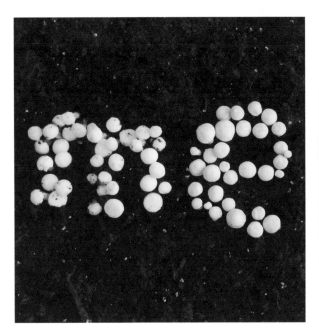

30th

principle

Designing (with) natural processes
Mushrooms made from modelling
clay and ice. The ice melts and frees
up space for something new.
Me becomes We becomes Them.

Cress, cat grass, and champignons
(growth period 3–4 weeks) come
next. In the end, nature completely
takes over.

"The project (a stop-motion film)
is an attempt to break down the
interpersonal relational level and the
relationship of humans to nature into
simple pictures."

→ Integrate natural phenomena
like wind and sun into your project.
Quick tip: Use pithy terms to
allow the viewer space for their
own thoughts.

Where our calculations fail,
that is what we call coincidence.

−ALBERT EINSTEIN

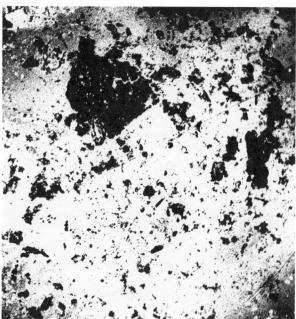

31st

principle

Poetics of chance

Does your music play in any order with the shuffle setting on your music player or do you configure your playlist meticulously? Coincidence or intention?

Context: The aim is to capture a transitory moment. A ball with adhesive tape rolls through the city and collects tiny particles. These serve as a template for concrete paving stones with the title "Footprint of a Metropolis". Set your individual parameters using a random process chosen in the form-finding process. Your tools and methods always influence the result: the apparatus with which you randomly collect something, the precise selection of things you encounter, and the criteria you use to choose something.

*You can be very wild
and still be very wise.*
−YOKO ONO

→ Bring poetics into your project
by attaching great importance to
something that may be completely
insignificant. Take something fragile,
impermanent, or small from your
project context as a prop for your
project's form finding or narrative.

Light

The ethereal material of light is a fantastical phenomenon. To explain it in more detail would need a few more pages. Photons – tiny particles and waves at the same time – shoot from the sun to the earth as daylight. If, for example, they strike our backs, they are for the most part absorbed and release heat. If they hit a white wall, most of them are reflected and shoot off again. When they hit water, it creates interference. We all know the beautiful way light refracts on the seabed. When you work with light, you try to have photons do what you want them to do. For this you need space and time. The choice of light source and its positioning, as well as that of the observer, the properties of your material, its surface texture, and your technical tools are your playthings here. Remember a great sentence that is sure to stay with you for a while: matter casts shadows.

In this chapter you will find suggestions on how to create shadows and integrate them into your project or how to simply capture light in motion in a time exposure. How to use transparency, translucency, and reflection to create a 3D impression with light. How light can fall, with what quality, whether it dazzles or is very soft. The examples also show you how you can use different colours from the light spectrum, artificial light, or daylight.

In the other chapters you will find additional food for thought:

Bundling light
Space / Zigzag → 122

Ambience
Space / Red → 121

Backlighting
Structure / Zoom cotton wool and sugar → 192
Time / Oil and water → 136

Drawing with light
Time / Curtain → 138

Fire as light source
Time / Pandemonium → 142

32nd
principle

Painting with light, time exposure
This requires a torch and a camera that allows you to set the exposure time manually or semi-manually. You don't even need a lens filter to take pictures in the dark. It only takes about 30 seconds to make a drawing. Just like Pablo Picasso's famous light drawings.

→ Give it a try with friends and have fun!

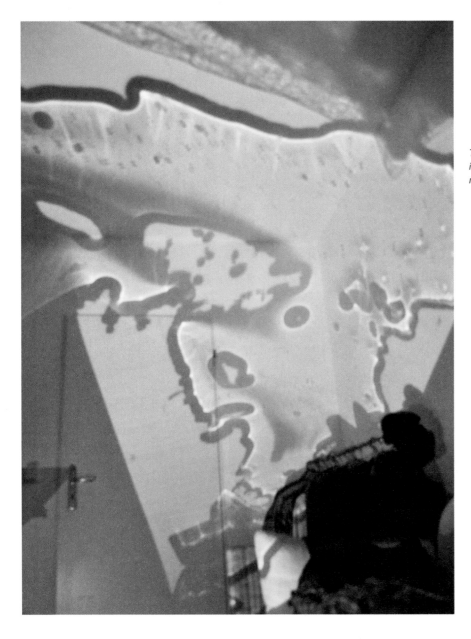

*The only thing I regret
in my life is never having
made comics.*

–PABLO PICASSO

33rd
principle

New forms through light refraction
Spread some water on the surface of an overhead projector and you will observe how new shapes are constantly being created. By translating and enlarging it in the space, you can see, upside down, what you might otherwise not see. As when reading clouds with friends, you interpret shapes differently depending on your mood or culture. Visual perception is visual thinking.

→ Light and chance harbour forms of script and signs for your project.

↓
futuristic
chain-linked
avant-garde
defamiliarised
dominant

34th
principle

Modelling surfaces with reflection
Some surfaces look fine, others do
not. The black polished surface of
a piano does, a shiny black garbage
bag doesn't. The matt aluminium

casing of the computer, yes ...
A space blanket is illuminated with
light. The folds are so aesthetic
that they would almost suffice for a
fashion shoot.

→ Photograph ordinary and less
sexy surfaces in a way that makes
them interesting and new for us.

transient

mirroring

positive-negative

critical

secluded

35th
principle

Achieving immersion with light in a small space

Even with a 40 × 60 cm box without any virtual reality (VR), it is possible to take viewers into another world. Creating a takeaway universe. With a little technology and sound, you can create a major effect in exhibitions with the tried-and-tested peep box. A box made of MDF (medium-density fibreboard), painted black, is equipped with a peephole. Inside there are planes of acrylic glass crossing diagonally at right angles. These surfaces and the inside of the box are covered with mirror foil. An LED light band runs inside the box. Different room and light situations are run with a micro-controller (Arduino). These are coupled with an audio track. They lead the viewer from a dazzled, short-sighted impression of the room into outer space. It is based on research into light smog.

→ The element of imperfection makes certain images appear realistic even when they are constructed. Body posture, image sequence, and sound work together to immerse the viewer as intensively as possible in your project for a few moments.

Light

↓
swelling
mutant
time-based
organic
bizarre

36th
principle

Using material properties in light
Process gelatin, bitter lemon, and liquid highlighter into a fluorescent material as part of a search for motifs for a campaign on future scenarios.

→ Illuminated with special light, for example black light, certain material properties become visible, such as fluorescence. Don't be afraid to develop your own material combination to suit your purposes.

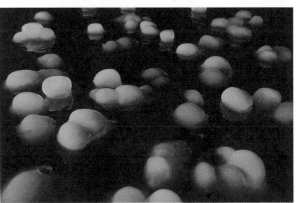

↓
objective
shadowy
illusory
distorted
high-contrast
(black-and-white)

37th
principle

Narrating with projection mapping

At some point you must have already seen how the shadow of a banister runs up the stairs in a graphic zigzag. The stairs are the substrate and the varying distance from the banister distorts the shadows that are cast. The principle of a heterogeneous substrate can be used in projection mapping. In various video sequences, faces and expressions are projected onto a face. The footage alternates between moving images and stills. In the moments in which the face as a substrate also moves, a narrative dynamic emerges that brings still images and illustrations to life. The boundaries between real space and

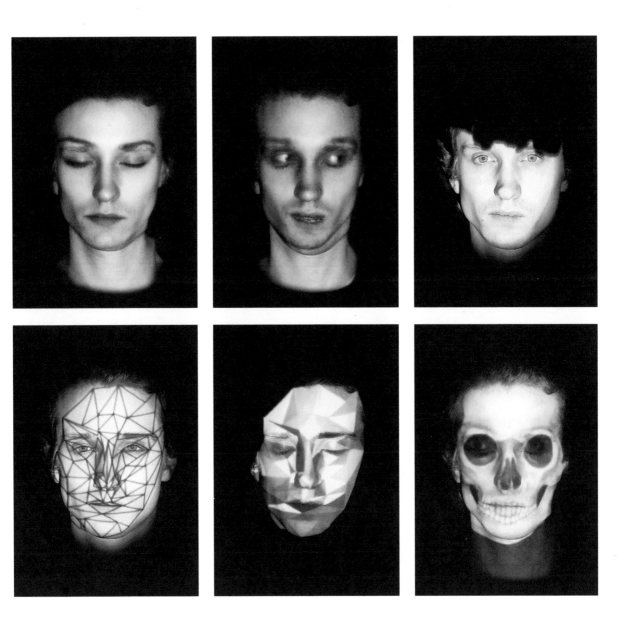

image space merge through light and time. The story told is based on Franz Schubert's *Winterreise*.

→ Start with an image editing program in which you set the mask by using the selection tool. Begin to assign like to like, which creates some particularly nice moments of confusion.

Note: A so-called "rainbow effect" can be caused by the overlapping of different frequencies. You can solve this problem by synchronising beamer, screen, and camera at 50 Hz.

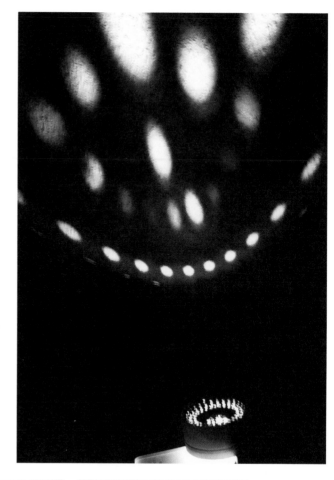

38th
principle

Ready-made

A cylindrical cardboard housing has a slot into which you insert your mobile phone. There are two drain strainers on the front of the housing, with colour foil clamped between them. When moved in opposite directions, the sieves serve as apertures and release rosettes of light in various configurations. The idea is to replace fiddling around on your mobile phone in bed with an atmospheric evening light that encourages healthy sleep.

→ You only need to provide the infrastructure for part of your project. Use semi-finished products and think about which components and infrastructure could be outsourced.

once

↓

illusionary

schematic

spatial

geometric

high-contrast

Light

Es ist schwer Menschen hinters Licht zu führen, sobald es ihnen aufgegangen ist.

It's easy to keep people in the dark until they've seen through you.

—ALFRED POLGAR (1873–1955)

39th

principle

Light as key

Where there is light, there is also shadow and vice versa. A coded statement is decoded through light. The message is hidden in the shadow. The viewer must first interactively find the correct angle of light incidence with a mobile phone torch in order to recognise a word. Based on the "Slow Reading" principle, they read their way word by word. Aluminium wire is easy to shape, without pliers or gloves. Here it is fastened to a wooden panel. Add shapes as a shadow!

→ Surprise viewers with the unexpected when the light comes on!

Light

↓
connections
network structure
distortion

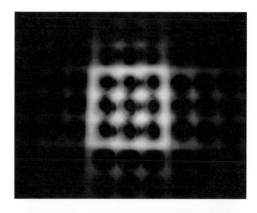

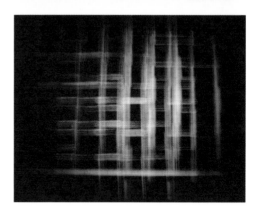

40th
principle

Superimposing shadows through several (simultaneous) light sources

Maybe you know the principle: When you walk from street light to street light in the dark ... The shadow in front gets smaller and smaller and the one behind catches up with every step. Project: An interactive black box to play with shadows falling on a sheet of acrylic glass. There are twenty-four torches on the bottom of the box. Handles on the side allow the interactive dynamic change of light patterns. A range of geometric templates is available. These templates are stretched on rubber. They can be manipulated in

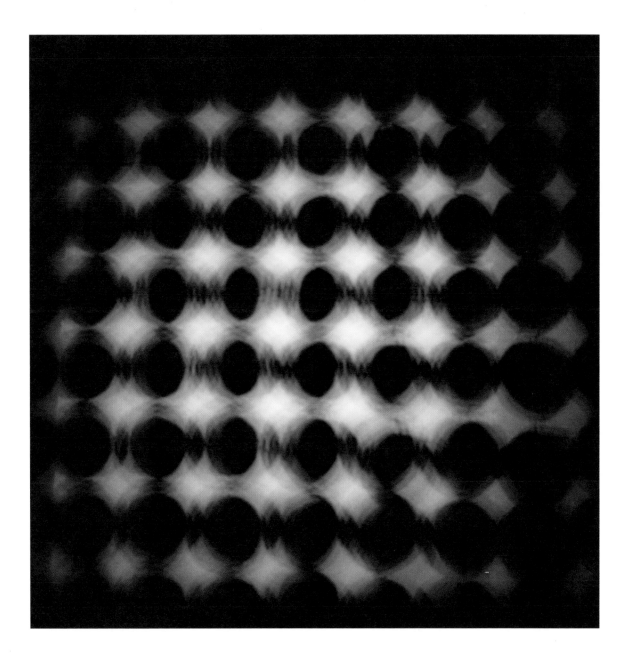

such a way that they distort and their distance from the light source varies, immediately resulting in a changing shadow image.

→ If the proportions of light and shadow distributed on a surface remain in balance, sometimes the light and sometimes the shadow will become a graphic element.

Note: As in the project "Room – Cotton bud" (→ 109), this form of box can also serve as a functional principle for creating and testing variants by working with templates.

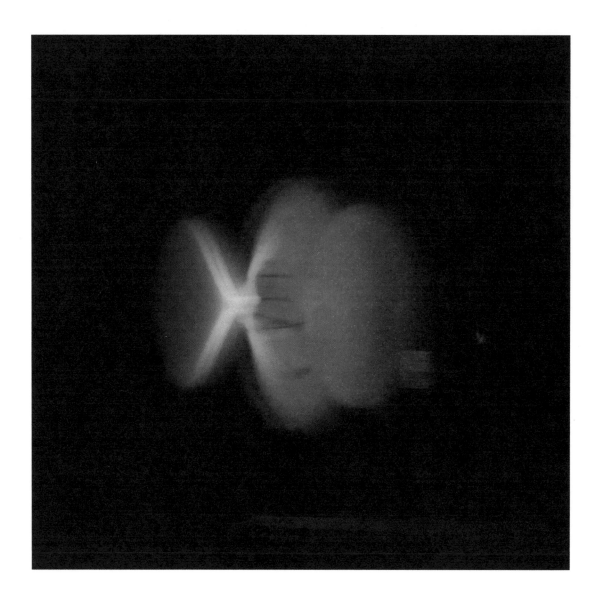

41st
principle

Capturing light with a time exposure
Study with bending lights in a hand mixer. Create beautiful progressions of colour with a time exposure of moving glow sticks, as the fluorescent colours overlap.

→ You can create gradients very quickly in Photoshop, but something so dynamic and 3D is special.

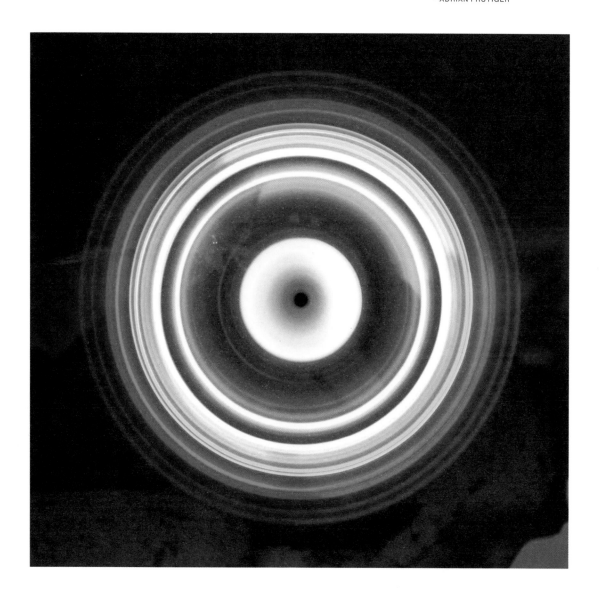

42nd

principle

Setting light points in motion
Study of sliding contacts with
LED. The bar with the lights on it is
powered by a drill. The photograph
that is taken in this case is not a time
exposure, because at this speed our
eye is able to assemble the dots into
a line.

↓

temporary

constructed

transformative

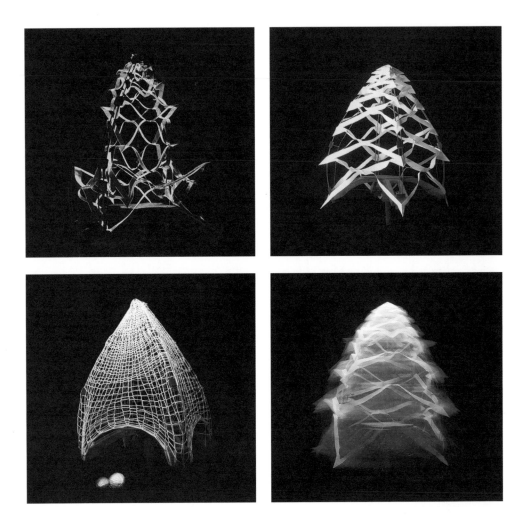

43rd

principle

Black light
Time exposure of rotationally symmetrical bodies
A substructure made of carbon fibre rods is driven by a drill. Grid structures made of paper, fabric, and string follow the centrifugal forces and produce unusual images with a time exposure. UV light (aka black light or UV-A) is also used to check banknotes.

→ Maybe you can use an X-ray aesthetic in your project or have something invisible appear under black light.

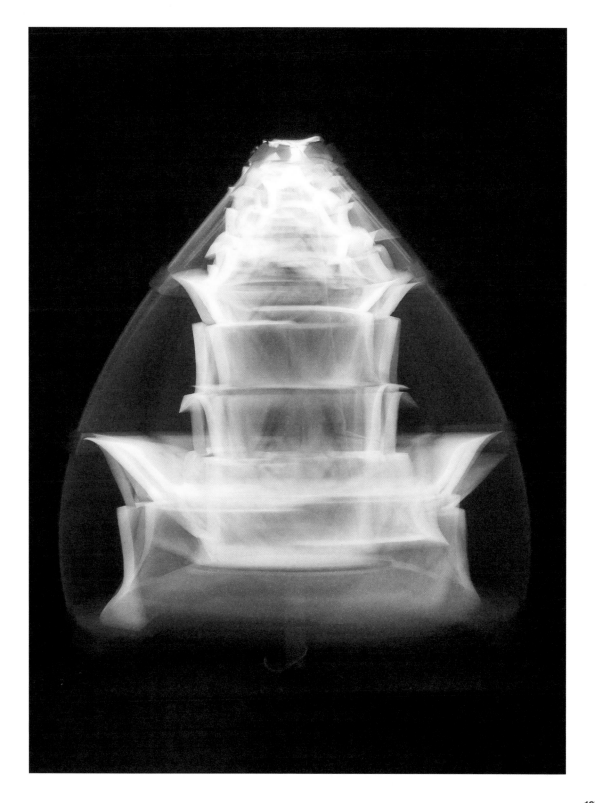

44th
principle

**Coloured shadows with
two light sources
Study of circular surfaces**
Tip: A flat composition is always clearer in black and white. Start by developing that and then move to colour. Circling light sources create semi-shadows (penumbra) of red and green light. The complementary contrast enhances the graphic effect. Coloured penumbra are created when only one colour is visible. We distinguish between complete shadows (umbra) and half shadows (penumbra). In a complete shadow with two light sources, both shadows overlap. It is black there. In a half-shadow, the shadow of one light source is coloured by the hue of the other.
Note: Sheets of coloured plastic in front of your normal light sources are sufficient.

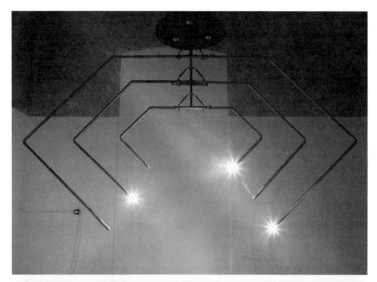

↓
perspective
shadow
repetition
rotation
interaction

45th
principle

Creating discomfort through light
Context: The principle of interrogation. Gyrating bright light. The aim was to stage a threatening situation with a revolving light. The adjustable motors on the ceiling underscore the mood with their technical noise.

→ This principle is applied in the exhibition context. For example, an unpleasant lighting atmosphere can be created to convey the experience of a story in a particularly emphatic way. You don't have to dazzle someone right away. You can also achieve a lot with an extremely cool lighting atmosphere.

NICHT JEDER HAT EINEN WARMEN PLATZ ZUM SCHLAFEN

Not everyone has a warm place to sleep.

46th

principle

Exploiting the light spectrum
Red light is part of the infrared
radiation from the solar spectrum.
We can perceive it with the naked

eye and it generates heat on the
human skin.
Context: Studies on red light are
transferred into a project with a

Berlin homeless people's association.
A campaign to tackle homelessness
is designed to stimulate dialogue
on the topic in public space and

social

physical

interactive

possibly generate donations. A young woman in a bathrobe stands in an automatic photo booth that looks like a Snow White coffin. She is freezing.

A passer-by's donation, put into a small box, activates the red light for a short time so that the woman gets warm.

→ Turn your project into a conversation starter.

Colour

The phenomenon of colour is directly linked to light. When we see colour, we see coloured light, or rather light stimuli, which are perceived in our retina together with other information from the brain as a hue.

The two basic principles of colour mixing, additive and subtractive, can be used as a design tool: additive, in places where colour shines as light; subtractive, for everything else, wherever colour is mixed, applied, printed, and is an integral element. The perception and meaning of colour vary between cultures. Nowadays, brides in China get married in white, whereas in the past they wore red.

How can I make my project even better with colour? In this section you will primarily find processes, principles, and tools for dealing with colour, as well as for applying and mixing colour as a material.

A few examples will show you what you could do with it now: using digital colour selection back and forth, selecting colour by means of programming, applying colour of whatever composition with every conceivable object, alienating the familiar or intensifying colour over time, working with overlays of transparent colour layers or being fascinated by the aesthetics of dissolving pigments in water. If you don't know which colour fits, see the funny side of it – as my professor Ron Arad used to say, with a twinkle in his eye, "If you can't make it good, make it big. If you can't make it big, make it red."

In the other chapters you'll find additional food for thought:

Bathing rooms in coloured light
Space / Red → 121

Coloured shadows
Light / Light rotor → 168

Impregnating with colour
Time / Deaf → 141

Colour changes
Space / Wax → 120

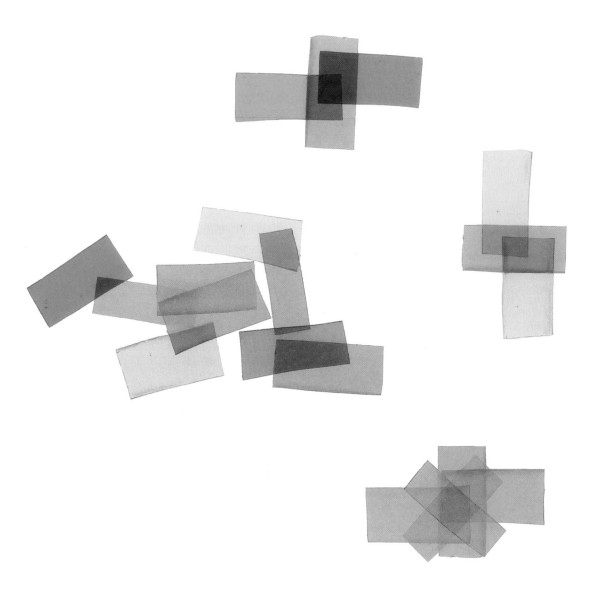

47th
principle

Subtractive colour mixing:
Mixing colours as with a brush
The superimposition of transparent colour surfaces also works according to this principle. Here, Tic Tac boxes are cut up.

→ When you arrange flat surfaces in an analogue way, you almost always get different results than on the computer. This applies to both colour and black and white. Use an intuitive and direct approach to composition.

Even flat sheets have a three-dimensional quality, which you can then work with photographically!

48th
principle

Colour in motion
Ferromagnetic toner is shaped with
a magnet on a wooden letter.

→ Let serifs go walkabout as
inspiration for new fonts!

49th

principle

Watching colour dissolve

I'm sure you know the magical moment when the bath essence is distributed in the water. Studies of the process of how colour dissolves in water as a stimulus to form finding.

Different colours are gradually infused or poured into a fish tank or bowl. In the example you see ink and acrylic paint in water, as well as milk in water, photographed under black light.

→ Discover figures, adopt different tempos in the dissolution process as inspiration or simply as a decorative aspect for possible designs for a pattern.

↓

dissolving

50th
principle

Make the tool yourself

DIY is in. The brush, which was originally hairy and intended for painting, takes on a new meaning. It can be adapted by knotting a balloon around around a pencil, transforming it into a gentle stamp. The round shape can be used to dab circles. Hair curlers work great for rolling.
→ The good old potato has great potential too! Pointillism and impressionism have produced fascinating images. Why not reinterpret it? Compose a drawing from many tiny elements. Concentrate repeated or varying shapes, colours, and sizes into lines and areas.

51st

principle

Analogue pixel graphics
Study of empty space: Coloured ink is injected into bubble wrap using a syringe.

→ Since the injecting is done point by point, this principle is also suitable for a stop-motion film. Any typography that comes out of this must then adapt to the grid.

52nd
principle

Caprice and volition

The picker is used in many colour-selection programs. We use it to choose from an area of colour. Or we enter numbers expressing colour values or move a few sliders. But you can also incorporate the element of chance and take a rather more conceptual view of colour selection by picking colours in a picture related to your project and then compiling a colour climate.

Note: You can use the Colour Wheel (Adobe Color CC) color.adobe.com to select colour families and tonal values.

→ If you want your photography to fit into the existing colour world of a corporate identity, reverse-engineering can be a help in determining tonal values and matching colours. Pick tones from existing photographs and colour scales and adjust your climate to them backwards, so to speak.

Neue Liebe, neues Leben

Herz, mein Herz, was soll das geben?
Was bedränget dich so sehr?
Welch ein fremdes, neues Leben!
Ich erkenne dich nicht mehr.
Weg ist alles, was du liebtest,
Weg, warum du dich betrübtest,
Weg dein Fleiß und deine Ruh –
Ach, wie kamst du nur dazu!

Fesselt dich die Jugendblüte,
Diese liebliche Gestalt,
Dieser Blick voll Treu und Güte
Mit unendlicher Gewalt?
Will ich rasch mich ihr entziehen,
Mich ermannen, ihr entfliehen,
Führet mich im Augenblick,
Ach, mein Weg zu ihr zurück.

Und an diesem Zauberfädchen,
Das sich nicht zerreißen läßt,
Hält das liebe, lose Mädchen
Mich so wider Willen fest;
Muß in ihrem Zauberkreise
Leben nun auf ihre Weise.
Die Verändrung, ach, wie groß!
Liebe! Liebe! laß mich los!

4865727a2c206d65696e204865
727a2c2077617320736f6c6c206
4617320676562656e3f0a57617
32062656472e46e67657420646
9636820736f20736568723f0a57
656c63682065696e206672656d
6465732c206e65756573204c65
62656e210a4963682065726b65
6e6e6520646963682062e696368
74206d6568722e0a5765672069
737420616c6c6c65732c20776173
206475206c696562746573743742c
0a5765672c20776172756d2064
7520646963682062062657472fc62
746573742c0a57656720646569
6e20466e6c6569df20756e642064
65696e6520527568201cc30a41
63682c207769656205206b616d73474
206475206e75722064617521

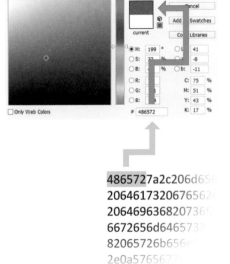

4865727a2c206d656
20646173206767656562
206469636820736f3
6672656d6d6464657
82065726b656
2e0a576565672

53rd

principle

Colour coding

Convert text into colour tones using hexadecimal code. Each letter and number has its own code in the hexadecimal system. The system uses sixteen specific characters, mostly the numbers 0–9 to represent the values from zero to nine and A, B, C, D, E, F to specify values from ten to fifteen. In the hexadecimal system, the word "hexadecimal" would produce the following series of characters: 4865786164656369d616c. This rule can also be applied to colours. Goethe's poem "Neue Liebe, neues Leben" is the starting point for an experiment examining the symbiosis of art and machine. The text is entered in the online hexadecimal converter. As a basic principle, colour values are entered in six-digit units into the Adobe Photoshop colour selection menu. Six consecutive

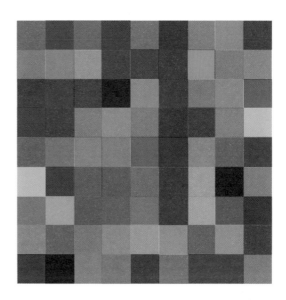

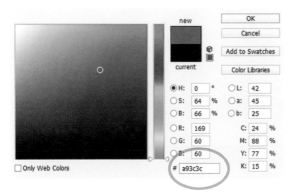

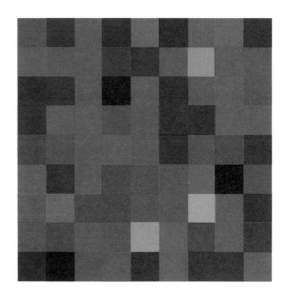

numbers are now entered into this field, so that the colour selection is determined numerically. This shade is transferred to a colour matrix of 9 × 9 squares. To make it brighter, the saturation of the image is set to 100%.

→ Find your own way to program colour. The net is full of converters, conversion programs for all kinds of purposes. Each letter has its own numeric code in the hexadecimal system. There are also binary code converters and so on. Try handing over responsibility for colour

selection to a system once in a while and then work with it from there.

Colour

↓
overlaid
gradated
coloured
organic
dynamic

54th
principle

Using an attractive colour
Transparent and opaque glycerine soap is melted with a soap dye and cut into new bars. The intense colour makes the soap pieces look like attractive gemstones.
Context: The students form a virtual "brainwashing committee", which gives away hundreds of these soaps in a public setting, to stimulate political dialogue even among people who are turned off by politics.

*Education is the most
powerful weapon ...*
—NELSON MANDELA

→ Use colours to make a material
exciting and to convey your message
to people.

→ Get out of the workplace and seek
out contact with people. If you have a
question, find out what other people
think!

55th
principle

Typology and culture of colour
Study on the spectrum of motifs used in banknotes in Europe (rough overall impression, without Swiss francs, for example). Variations in population

contingent on different living conditions are natural in the plant and animal kingdoms. Typologies and taxonomies allow comparisons to be drawn. Use colour as a cultural asset.

Study the colours and motifs of other cultures. Banknotes are strictly protected, so only small details can be used.

56th
principle

No colour

The depth of a lake is translated into different spatial models. The choice of colours changes from the classic colour spectrum of a geographic key to deep blue to shades of grey and finally to the colourless. The model is made of transparent straws.

→ Reduce your palette to a few colours, especially if the role of colour in your project is still unclear. Structures are good alternatives.

Colour

↓

spatial
abstract
high-contrast
bright

57th
principle

Projecting colour transparencies
The light beams of two slide projectors are refracted by polycarbonate plates protruding from a corner of a room at an angle of 45 degrees. The image motifs then also reflect onto the wall in the opposite corner. Additive colour mixing creates multiple transparencies extending all the way to white light. A staggered sequence puts emphasis on the process of superimposition.

Project context: The aim is to stimulate the discourse on stereotypical gender roles. Superimpositions should create room for in-between spaces with scope for interpretation.

↓

colorful

organic

provocative

feminist

58th
principle

The human reference

The airbrushed silicone casts of mandarins, avocados, and pears turn fruit and vegetables into body-like structures. The avocado's magnificent head of hair has a very special aesthetic. There are many hairy plants or wrinkly fruits and vegetables, but hardly any skin-coloured ones. It's fine if it's disorientating! This is a colour that is immediately assigned to us humans.

Structure

As with any physical artefact, structure refers to how something is "built up" from within: it is a multidimensional phenomenon. Its function can be aesthetic or constructive. If it is intellectual, it creates concepts. In most cases, the composition of a structure continues on the surface, so that the structure is a visible design feature. We can often draw conclusions about the structure of an object from its surface. This works well with a brick wall but not with a vacuum cleaner, and with data structures only if transparency is desired.

If you develop a structure or work with changing structures, it's a dynamic process. The form and its components are dependent on each other, since the structure helps to shape the whole.

Structure is redolent of clear thinking, order, and stability. Nowadays the word crops up in the political context because the whole society is experiencing structural change.

This chapter is about how we design a physical structure. What can we create a structure from? You can find existing structures and edit them for your purposes or create something special if you find an intriguing structure. How you create and arrange things determines the structure and surface. Connect things in an unusual way. Create fixed, movable, detachable connections, e.g. using force-fit, form-fit, or material bonding. You will need some tools, adhesives, cords, rubber bands. You might also use a technical device. Pretty much anything you can get your hands on is good. Particularly well suited are things that you can get hold of quickly, inexpensively, and in large quantities.

I would like to encourage you to approach digital processes and interfaces in a manner that is just as carefree and uninhibited as the way you plundered the refrigerator for experimental purposes in one of the previous chapters. Develop your very own approach to digital and analogue devices – your own set of rules even. There are multiple programs you can use to generatively develop design proposals, in both 2D and 3D. This also applies to designing structures and constructing things. The principle of the algorithm is much the same everywhere and has many different uses, though you have to get the hang of it first. However, you don't need any knowledge of programming to generate your own set of rules. You can do that working in analogue. It is only the rule-based repetition of a step that leads you from the simple to the complex. Just like cell division.

Explore the possibilities the hardware offers you. Explore devices – 3D printers, copiers – or just hack the code of the talking parrot. Find the limits of what is possible and develop your own methodology. You don't have to convert the refrigerator into a printer. Though why not? Some food is already printed.

Everything can be of service to you. A mishmash of analogue, digital, and iterative. Question everything. No process, program, or interface is fixed. Believe in yourself! (Examples of digital structures → 119, → 209)

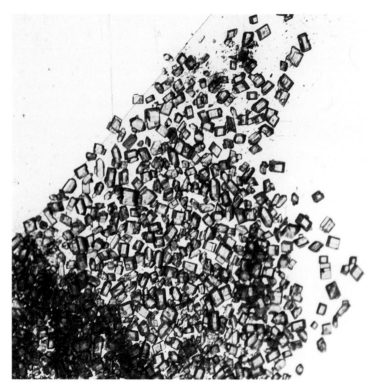

59th
principle

Zoom with the macro lens

If you photograph enlarged materials with a macro lens, you get intriguing structures. When you don't give viewers any indicators as to the size of the material, the image remains mysterious. If the material is backlit, this inverts the brightness. Our habitual way of seeing colour – which says that sugar (just above) and cotton wool (above right) are white – is undermined. Sugar is cast in a new light. The individual lumps are translucent, almost transparent. The refraction of light makes the crystal sugar look like precious stones. The dimensioning is suspended. The structures have attained an excessive degree of abstraction. Now they can serve for your visualisation. With the help of the macro lens,

↓
fusing

a string bag turns into a green organic mass.

Baking a rather different biscuit: Fresh sheets of lasagne are cut into strips and placed on a plate during baking. The flat organic mass takes on a 3D organic shape.

→ Use a diffuse light source if you have backlighting. Observe materials in close-up as you stack, line up, overlay, layer, twist, or fuse them. For once, follow geometric arrangement principles.

Study on the project → **204**

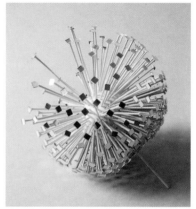

60th
principle

From unicellular to multicellular organisms

Hundreds of cable ties connected in loops create an object reminiscent of a sea urchin. At the slightest touch, the flexible movements of the individual zip ties bring the creature to life. Curves or tensioned surfaces can be modelled. Nylon tights – streched over the arms of corkscrews – adapt to the shape or give it volume. Hundreds of toothpicks are cast in plaster, creating a chaotic structure. A disco ball with wooden skewers becomes

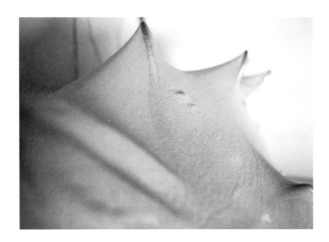

an object that looks a bit like an
animal. It seems to explode from the
centre with each mirror facet aligned
perpendicularly to the core.

→ Use a natural appearance to throw
people off. This allows you to work
dynamically as well without harming
any living beings.

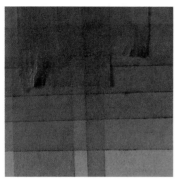

61st

principle

Staging transitions: The unstable structure
An organic structure is staged by dramatic body positions. Tempera, acrylic, fire varnish, Sellotape, Scotch tape, ink. A study sets out to develop the interior of a compact structure as a design feature. The pattern is developed in symbiosis with the human body, as the structure is unstable. The motif is to be used for a record cover.

fusing

staging

→ Create an object that requires at least one counterpart to function, such as membrane and structure or skin and bone. Create a system in which several actors interact with one another.

62nd

principle

**The whole is more than
the sum of its parts**

The individual piece as a structuring element (puzzle principle). The individual component in a grid. Temporary installation with political statement on gentrification. Delicate sound and metallic chink in the wind oppose the imminent din of the building site.

The fence serves merely as a putative grid. The metal plates, derived from a spatula, hang on a fine fabric.

→ Elicit a special sound from the movement of a structure. Every single element in your project can reflect light and create sound.

playful

interactive

transient

63rd

principle

The variable component
Polyhedra (polygons) made of plaster
can be designed variably and take
on any number of forms when they
are put together. A resource for
typographers and messages?

→ Cluster your building blocks
regularly or irregularly. Create a
closed surface from many small
elements.

64th

principle

**Structure with a natural function:
Mimicry and mimesis**
An animal's (poisonous) sting is
primarily designed for protection and
defence. Camouflage is protection

against being eaten or a means to
sneak up on one's own prey unseen.
Geometric basic forms become a
hi-vis vest as a concept fashion
(for women's rights, for example).

Flexible plastic tubes are threaded
together according to the principle
of geodesic triangles (Buckminster
Fuller). Pulling on the cord creates a
ridge of "stings".

Inspired by research on mimicry, a structure is developed and printed on fabric. Foreground and background merge.

→ Make it your task to find interpretations for contemporary ways of deploying protective mechanisms in the context of face tracking. You can explore the right to informational self-determination – also known as data protection – cybermobbing, data theft, and the digital shadow that we leave behind every day while surfing.

Structure

↓

(in)visible
measurable
luminescent

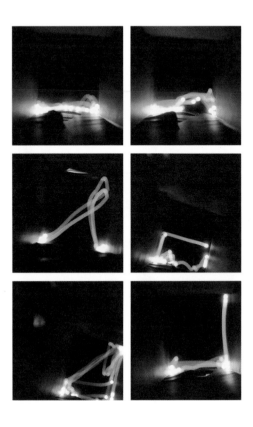

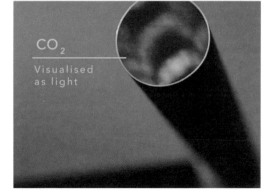

CO$_2$
Visualised
as light

*It is harder to crack
prejudice than an atom.*
—ALBERT EINSTEIN

65th
principle

**Obtaining a shape
through abstraction**
The variable triangular shape of a
light comes from the alternating
direction of movement of a molecule
flying through the air. You are
probably familiar with the nuclear
science logo with the three ovals.

The molecule changes direction as
soon as it hits an object or another
molecule. The form is in three
parts because a carbon dioxide
molecule consists of three atoms:
one of carbon and two of oxygen.
The formal-aesthetic element is an
essential factor in the design project.

In a preliminary study, the movement
of a marble on the route of the Berlin
S-Bahn ring was observed.
→ Have a look at the natural
sciences, they are a rich source of
inspiration.

66th
principle

Same-same but different: Variants
The joints of a luminaire can be used to create different forms. Candles go out as soon as the oxygen content in the air ceases to feed the flame. Normally, a light does not go out when there's trouble in the air. In this project it does. Etymologically, the saying comes from the war: there's bomb smoke in the air.

When the enemy is gone, the air is clear – breathe a sigh of relief. The project context is working with light. An air sensor and LEDs inside are controlled by an Arduino board. You measure the CO_2 content, and the light goes out when it reaches a certain value. If the value recovers, the LEDs light up again. So, give the place a good airing.

→ Combine commercially available sensors that respond to pressure, position, temperature, or oxygen with vibration motors, LEDs, or sounds and discover a range of new fields of application.
→ Use joints and hinges for a wealth of variants in the presentation.

Structure

↓
delimited
textural
recycling
fusing

67th
principle

Structuring through fusion
Lozenges in two sizes made of TetraPak are ironed onto masking film. The coating melts the two materials together, creating a

colourful graphic pattern on the inside. The gaps become transparent hinges. The project context is to create a physical shell.

→ Stage structures with light. Stage the design in context for the documentation of your project.

Preliminary studies → 193

68th

principle

The sand form

Here the fine-concrete lamp is defined by its polygonal surface structure. The negative form for it, made from polypropylene, looks the same, only the other way around. This is the positive-negative functional principle. Studies of the colour shade of the plaster mass with pigments mixed in.

Note: Everything that is poured into the mould must also be removed again. Bevelled, flexible, or multi-part moulds enable complex casting processes. Think about these early on in the project.

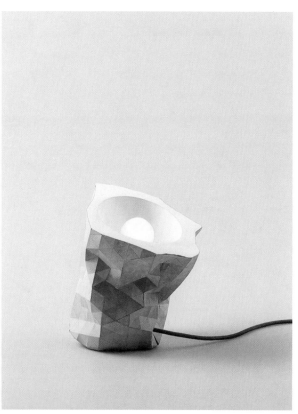

→ In fashion, seams are often
a design element, whether they
represent a colour contrast or are
inverted. Where can the inside
become the outside in your project?

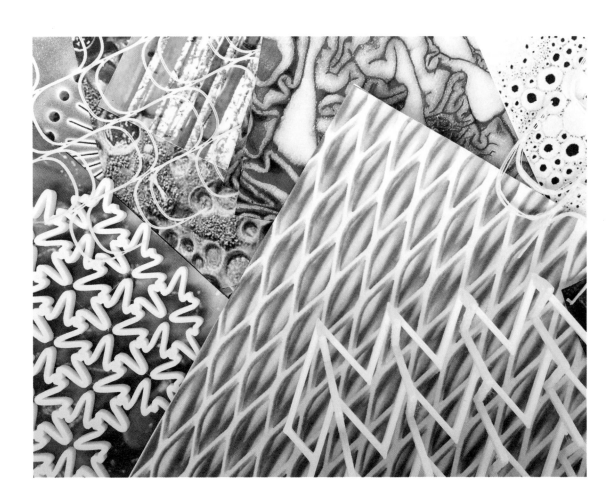

69th

principle

Developing the structure

A 3D printed object developed from solid and flexible material properties. The "less is more" approach also applies to 3D printing – with maximum stability. The less material is used, the shorter the printing time. The world's first 3D printed hockey glove came out of structural studies. The hand part is made of "NinjaFlex". The back of the hand is protected by an extra "PLA" attachment.

image above: Experimental studies of natural and fabricated structures.

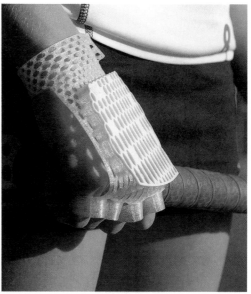

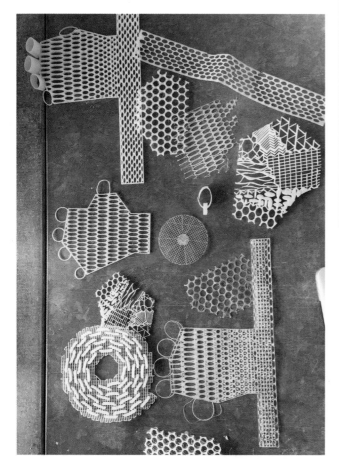

image above: Studies of manipulation possibilities in the printing process, prototypes, and revision (iteration) of the model with different materials.

→ Try to reduce the number of connections in your project and incorporate them into the objects. The 3D printer allows a new variety of shapes in which individual elements are not bound to (DIN) standards in order to be connected. Think about the linkage right away to save on resources. Create an efficient use of materials through intelligent new structures.

Material

What material should I use? How can I process it?

Material is what a thing is made of. In many cases, we only look for an adequate – possibly the cheapest – material to implement our designs. But if we start with the material itself, it can inspire us and give us new ideas. Everyone is in a position to do material research and develop a material. In principle, it can be anything: photographs, pictures, or video footage. Your material in the current project can also be a semi-finished product, the small and inconspicuous things that you have all around you and which have specific properties and functions. Just ask yourself: What else can this thing do? As my mentor Vico Magistretti taught me, "Look at the usual with an unusual eye."

In this section you will find principles about what can be viewed as material, how you can use and stage its creation or decay for your design, as well as examples that utilise specific material properties (Time/Oil → **136**) and show how semiotics and the level of interpretation of material aesthetics underscore their message. You can use plastics or organic and natural materials and draw on their sensuality, sound, aesthetics, haptics, or specific properties. Does it burn? Does it deform? Is the material digital?

In this third section of the book, you can regard everything as material. So here is just a brief reference to two other projects that use the technical procedure of manufacturing or material processing as a design principle (Structure/3D printing → **209**) or take the transition of aggregate states as an exciting moment in the narrative (Time/Ice → **140**).

Quick tip
to get you
started:

**Paper is
amazingly
versatile.**

MaterialDistrict.com is
an informative website
with newsletters about
materiality.

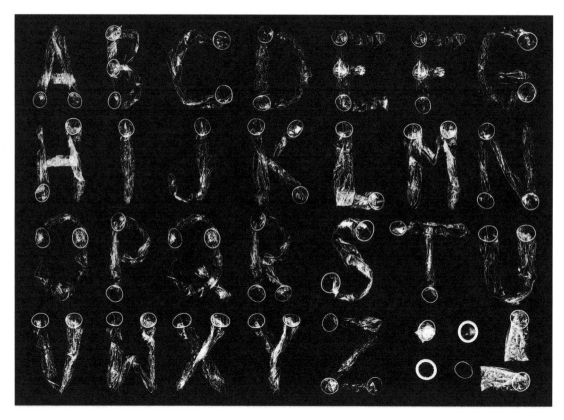

70th

principle

Take a material out of its context/ semantic level and then put it back
Study of the structure and materiality of an object as a way of emphasising its characteristics. The "Feeling Ultra Sensitive" condom typography is based on the transparency of

the material and its ability to reflect light. Latex condoms are placed on a copier with the lid open. The font should transmit feelings and discreetly reflect the product characteristics. You can definitely see it as part of an AIDS campaign, right?

→ Look for old technologies and devices such as a black-and-white copier that you can use to invert copy masters to discover something new. Flexible and transparent materials are particularly suitable here.

71st

principle

**Imitate something similar
at the level of content**
Cigarette cotton filters are bound
together as blossoms with wire.
The filter material is made up of
fibres arranged lengthwise, which
are pressed into a cylindrical shape.

With the new level of association,
the filters are borrowed from their
original context and transferred back
into a new form, which in turn can
recall the context.
→ Work like Marcel Duchamp. Make
a readymade. You can do this, for

example, by taking semi-finished
products like a zipper. A zipper
becomes jewellery, cotton buds
become an architectural model,
cotton filters become cherry
blossom …

Material

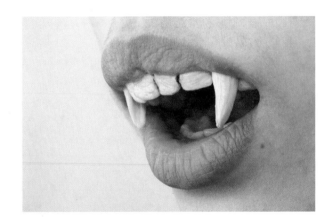

72nd
principle

Structure and fibres of natural materials: Study of nature
Study nature! Let yourself be guided by the observation, drawing, and dissection of the structure of fibres, fruits, and tubers in your design. While analysing the structure of

garlic, the student discovered that garlic is easy to carve. The design of a set of false teeth would certainly not please Count Dracula.
The chalice-like structure of the artichoke serves as inspiration for a trophy.

→ The observation of mechanisms in living creatures in nature has resulted in a variety of innovations in bionics. Find a material property or movement that you can transfer into your project.

Humour is by far the most significant activity of the human brain.
— EDWARD DE BONO

73rd
principle

Material and semiotics
Semiotics is the theory of signs and their meaning. When you design a pictogram, you must constantly check its readability. And this can vary depending on the culture. A material in combination with a sign always influences the level of meaning. There is a lovely adage: "Visual perception is visual thinking", which boils down to "You see what you think". The nice thing about there being scope for interpretation is that you leave up to others what they see. You just show a balloon that's been cut open.

→ When you design a graphic symbol, think about how it will be oriented. Will you allow it to be turned upside down or not? Check possible ambiguities to avoid conflicts or indeed to create scope for interpretation.

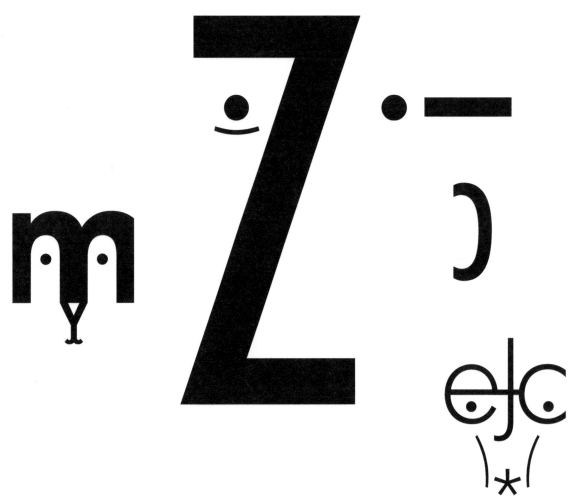

74th
principle

Letters and glyphs as material
Faces are made recognisable. A material can be anything you lay hands on. This is a plea for the art of paper cutting and the snipping and pushing that goes with it. If the letters were constantly there on the table, everyone would have already made a figure out of them. Faces are among the most easily recognisable signs in our environment, because our perception processes the horizontal lines in them phenomenologically, like performing scan. Two dots and a mouth, done. That's how little you need to identify a face. The letters have to be outsmarted here as their tendency is always to get us reading them. Ideally, as with some structures, you create maximum abstraction, for example, by flipping them, before you use them.

→ Where did you last see a face – in a cloud, a tree trunk, a house façade? If you draw a blank, go on a quick three-minute search!

75th
principle

Change of perspective: The human body as a source of inspiration
Folds in the skin can have a lot to say. About other people or about themselves. Here a typography is created by the in-between spaces. The photos are vectorised and transferred to black and white.

Tattooing, scratching, painting. The skin is the largest organ we humans have. Stefan Sagmeister became famous for provocatively carving type into his own skin as an invitation text. I don't want you to hurt yourself: Painting your body is also exciting.

→ The quantified self is the trend towards self-measurement to optimise performance and quality of life. Why not develop your own personal alphabet? Metadata, likes, GPS data, or skin folds, everything has potential. With more or less conversion work.

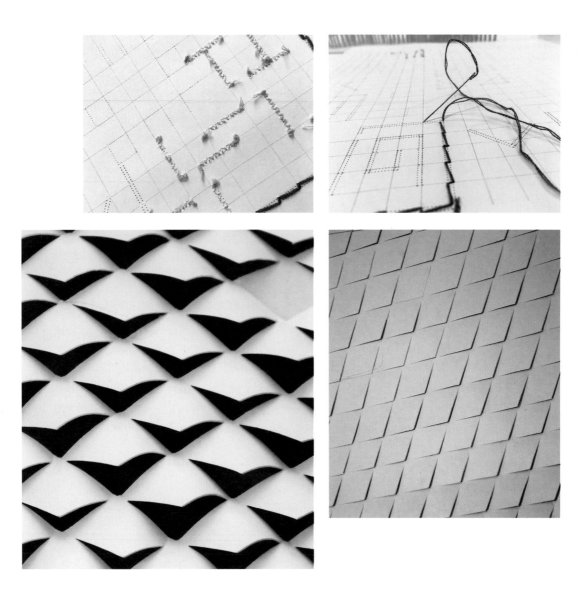

76th
principle

Paper is patient
Using the spectrum of
material properties
Paper is slit and opens when pulled. The study was created to develop

a lampshade that the user can adjust to vary the light output.
When you sew lines to create a unique sensual aesthetic, you get a special kind of architectural

layout drawing. Certainly not something for everyday presentations, but for a special occasion.

AMNESTY MACHT SICHTBAR
Amnesty makes visible

AMNESTY MACHT SICHTBAR
Amnesty makes visible

77th

principle

Interaction with the material
The principle of steganography. Citric acid reacts (thermally) to heat. The message requires interaction for it to be decoded (→ 161).
Context: Concept sketch for a campaign for Amnesty International

(AI). Amnesty stands for bringing light into darkness and making the invisible (injustice) visible.

→ This process of change only works once with citric acid. Thermochromic colours can change back to their original colour. Subtle messages can also be communicated with related principles such as scratch pictures, possibly made of wax.

78th
principle

High tech + low tech

OLEDs (organic light emitting diodes) backlight the chambers of multilayer corrugated board. The digital-looking pixel typography produced in this way shows individual words that visitors can combine into sentences in an interactive installation. The optional statements such as "Siri is a smart witch" serve to stimulate discourse on new technologies.

→ Don't hesitate to associate the qualities of simple materials with new technologies, especially when prototyping.

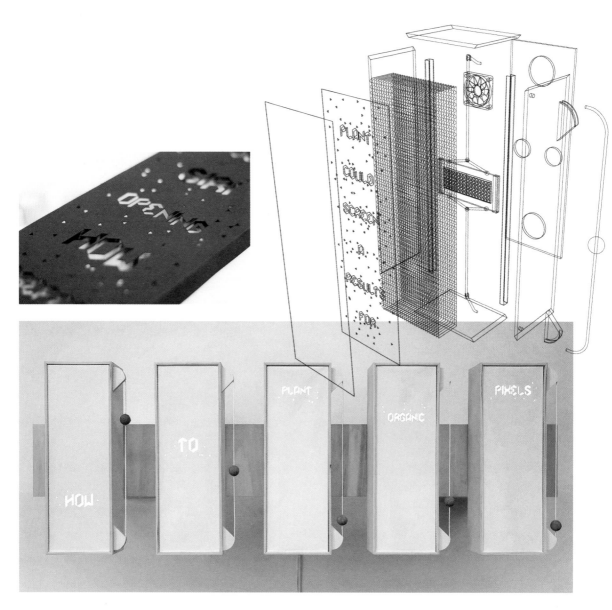

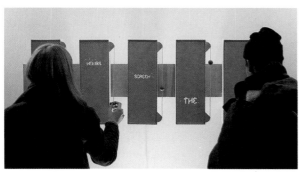

The new always happens against the overwhelming odds of statistical laws and their probability, which for all practical, everyday purposes amounts to certainty; the new therefore always appears in the guise of a miracle.

—HANNAH ARENDT

Material

↓

loud – silent
organic – geometric
irritation
2D/3D/4D

  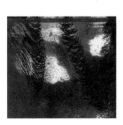 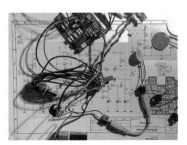

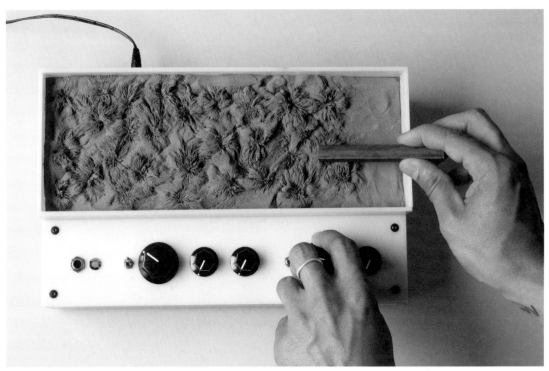

79th
principle

Creating sound experiences through interaction with a material
Iron powder is put on a copper plate. Magnets are placed underneath it, causing the powder to rise.

Piezo pickups below the copper plate become a microphone. Every movement can be perceived and made audible by the piezos. The result is an experimental musical instrument with five potentiometers. Acrylic glass and concrete form the housing.

→ Create artefacts that use material behaviour visually or sensorially!

80th
principle

Mapping materials

The orange, its peel, mesocarp, and pulp serve as masters. In a 3D program, the surfaces, texture and structure of the citrus fruit are modelled and processed as digital material, sculpting, shading, and texturing Nike Jordan 1.

→ When it goes digital, create surfaces and materials for models yourself!

Material   ↓

camouflaged
overgrown
additive
predominant

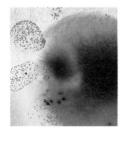

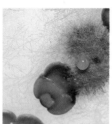

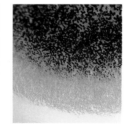

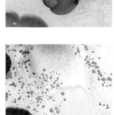

81st
principle

Aesthetics of mould:
Cultivating material
Mould as a source of inspiration. On the one hand, bacterial colonies and fungi are undesirable; on the other, mysterious and beautiful. Project: Prints are taken from different persons as bacterial samples. These are used to inoculate agar matrices, which are incubated and kept warm over a period of days. Visually inspired by the material, a decorative element is created. In this way, skin bacteria are conceptually returned to their place of origin.

→ Bred and grown structures

provide a rich spectrum of colour and composition. Draw on this for your design!
Note: Petri dishes already filled with a substrate for cultivating microorganisms are available in laboratory shops. Casein soy and peptone agar are also suitable.

82nd

principle

Displaying a material

Hotplates under an aluminium plate and ice with plant remains on a metal chain abstract a complex process. Permafrost thaws as the earth's temperature rises, releasing methane gas that enters the atmosphere and intensifies the warming process.

Project context: The artists Fischli & Weiß and Roman Signer are sources of inspiration for visual experiments on tipping points in climate change. In cooperation with the Potsdam Institute for Climate Impact Research, students work experimentally to visualise a series

of tipping points in the Earth system (vimeo.com/363540500). You can also develop models of a material or prototype material.

→ Make use of the abstraction potential of models.

83rd

principle

**Aesthetically staging the decay
and splicing of a material**
Using the banana as an example,
the transience of the original joint is
staged.

→ A banana tattoo can be used to
exploit the transience of the material.
Draw or write with an empty ballpoint
pen on the surface and wait a few
days.

↓
metamorphosis
defective
erosion
aesthetic
processing

84th
principle

Developing material: Aesthetically staging the destruction and transformation of a material
Allowing mistakes or leaving out minor corrections leads students to develop a material that does not yet exist: latex-covered paper. It is systematically staged in a video.

→ Enjoy the potential that gaps, mistakes, unforeseen events, and irregularities offer you. Make a conscious decision to stage them.

Index

Annex

The origin of the method

As a tool kit for creativity and inspiration, the 5D method has undergone a very special development process. I will review the context and the interwoven strands of content for you here. The starting point of the method is an approach that has a long tradition in the teaching of design at university level. In this method, students analyse the work of an artist, a designer, or an architect and develop an independent work based on their findings. I learned this method myself in my design studies at the Berlin University of the Arts a good twenty-five years ago. Having drawn lots, I was assigned fashion designer Yoji Yamamoto and developed a project in a small team in homage to him. The result was a kinetic floating object consisting of ten black interconnected surfaces. Each surface had a particular shape and the whole ensemble bobbed up and down, responding to impulses received from the small wave movements. It was meant to evoke Yamamoto's play with silhouettes and drapery.

I have been teaching design at art colleges and universities for designers for fifteen years. I took up the traditional "homage" method and systematised it further. Generations of students from art and media studies, architecture and urban planning, interface design, communication design, and industrial design have worked with this method for inspiration. Each generation refined the method so that it now has its place in this book, where you can call on all its different facets and get to know how it

works. Enriched by conversations with my colleague Professor Gabi Schillig, I have kept developing the method. I have adopted the division into three phases from her. Professor Wolfgang Jonas was a helpful sparring partner in the process of refining the idea. In addition, some important key insights from research into techniques of creativity and innovation research flow into the method for inspiration. In the analysing phase, you create analogies in the form of visualisations. Analogies transfer insights from one domain to another. In innovation research, they are ascribed to divergent thinking and heuristics, the "art of discovery". Here I make a further differentiation into the transformative thinking that allows you to think spatially between image, line, and space. The material laboratory is the phase in which you become a productive inventor. Inventing is a creative process of generating knowledge. It is based on iterative cycles of evaluation. You try something out, evaluate it, and continue. Failure is part of the process. Inventors ignore past experiences and give up previous knowledge. Chance plays a significant role in inventing, but not in a haphazard fashion.[92] In bringing together the steps, the synthesising phase, aspects of planning, work organisation, and marketing are added – because at a certain point every designer becomes an entrepreneur.

Last but not least, the method format originates from my own practice as a designer. In my independent work and in the design office MARTINI, MEYER I have conceived and realised interiors, design, and communication in the form of prestigious company rooms, products, and corporate identities. My natural propensity to see spaces in lines, develop scenarios from concepts, and rethink images into processes and sensory experience is extremely helpful. With this book I offer you the opportunity to enjoy these experiences for yourself and train your inspirational power. Designers identify niches and connect new things. In the meantime, most people know that design does not mean beautification. Creatives make a relevant contribution to the important questions of our time. Clever content comes across better when it is well packaged; we can and should make use of that. The role of design itself will also develop logically. The probing and questioning of all possible structures and processes – in politics, administrative settings, urban development, globalisation, and the management of scarce resources – is now vital. Designers use a wide variety of methods to create. The fact that this takes place together with other disciplines is an inherent part of design.

I hope you will enjoy adding to your personal wealth of experience and using it to generate new designs that are both exciting and responsible.

Theory and practice are friends. If you feel like deepening your theoretical knowledge, design theorists are just as important and inspiring as other creative people, scientists, and researchers. They lead the current discourse on developments, reflecting and positioning the working methods and strategies of designers in the light of social contexts. They locate design in scientific and creative research. They analyse the process of creating, thinking, and gaining knowledge and insight, as Wolfgang Jonas describes it, "through design, in design, with design and about design".[93] Bruce Archer, Gui Bonsiepe, Uta Brandes, Nigel Cross, Christopher Frayling, Gesche Joost, Tomás Maldonado, Claudia Mareis, Marshall McLuhan, Donald Schön, Richard Sennett, and Bruce Sterling have given me a great deal to take home with me, in lectures, as colleagues or presidents of the schools I studied at. Their intellectual models make it easier for you to locate yourself as a researching, practising designer. The list can be extended to include closely related disciplines such as sociology, anthropology, philosophy, cultural studies, architecture, and natural sciences. Here there are four thinkers and writers, in particular, who have stimulated and stretched me: Roland Barthes, Susan Sontag, Gaston Bachelard, and Walter Benjamin.

Endnotes

1   Daheim and Wintermann 2016.
2   Gillian Crampton Smith, lecture delivered on 23 May 2014, when she was awarded an honorary professorship in design at the University of Applied Sciences Potsdam.
3   Mieg 2010.
4   Medeiros 2017.
5   Pfeffer 2014.
6   Acoustics n.d.
7   Tubik Studio 2018.
8   Doorey 2019.
9   Analysis n.d.
10 Anthropocene n.d.
11 Klein 2017. See also Poli 2009.
12 Boeree 1991.
13 Oxford University Press (OUP) 2019a.
14 Medeiros 2017.
15 Searle 1980: 417.
16 Bézier curve n.d.
17 Cloud computing n.d.
18 Assmann 2009.
19 Oxford University Press (OUP) 2019b.
20 Communication n.d.
21 Goodwin and Duranti 1992: 3.
22 EPEA 2016.
23 EPEA 2016.
24 Creative Commons 2019.
25 Dunne and Raby 2007.
26 Cultural code n.d.
27 Cultural mapping 2017.
28 Clark, Sutherland, and Young 1995.
29 German Advisory Council on Global Change (WBGU) 2019: 12.
30 Vogt 2013.
31 Database n.d.
32 Empirical research n.d.
33 Entrepreneurship n.d.
34 Van der Waerden and Taisback 2019.
35 See Cognitive Space n.d.
36 See Schmidt 2012: 57.
37 "Manches, das heute noch als experiment wirkt, wird morgen als norm gelten." Bill 2008: 30.
38 Biyani 2013.
39 Heuristic n.d.
40 See Mieg 2010.
41 Human-centered design n.d.
42 DIN Standards Committee Ergonomics 2011.
43 WIPO n.d.
44 Intellectual Property 2017.
45 Social interaction n.d.
46 Interactivity n.d.
47 See Interfacedesign n.d.
48 The Editors of Encyclopaedia Britannica 2012.
49 Fraunhofer n.d.
50 Iteration n.d.
51 See Mieg 2010.
52 Laboratory n.d.
53 See Näger 2007: 11.
54 Digital literacy n.d.
55 Gamp and Gschwend 2017.
56 Christensson 2006.
57 Oxford University Press (OUP) 2019c.
58 Mockup n.d.
59 See Modell n.d.; The concept of model n.d.
60 Obsolescence n.d.
61 Parameter 2018.
62 See Noë 2006: 164.
63 Noë 2013.
64 Haptic perception n.d. See also Weber 1851.
65 Pictogram n.d.
66 Preset n.d. See also Default (computer science) n.d.
67 Process n.d.
68 Public value n.d.
69 Bott, Grassl, and Anders 2013: 243.
70 See Hintikka 2019.
71 See Schön 1983.
72 Research n.d.
73 Intermediate good n.d.
74 Semiotics n.d.
75 Service design n.d.
76 Strategy n.d.
77 Oxford University Press (OUP) 2019d.
78 System n.d.
79 See Haff 2014.
80 Norman 2016.
81 Cooper, Reimann, and Cronin 2007: XXVII.
82 Romero-Tejedor and Van den Boom 2013: 69.
83 Virtuality (philosophy) n.d.
84 Virtuality (disambiguation) n.d.
85 Virtual reality n.d.
86 Oxford University Press (OUP) 2019e.
87 Wizard of Oz experiment n.d.
88 See Merholz and Skinner 2016: 135–154, esp. 138.
89 Sheppard, Sarrazin, Kouyoumjian, and Dore 2018.
90 See Maldei, Koole, and Baumann 2019.
91 See Müller 2017.
92 Lemelson-MIT Program 2003: 28–32.
93 Jonas 2012: 34.

Literature list

Acoustics. (n.d.). In *Wikipedia*. Retrieved October 25, 2019, from https://en.wikipedia.org/w/index.php?title=Acoustics&oldid=919779766

Analysis. (n.d.). In *Wikipedia*. Retrieved October 25, 2019, from https://en.wikipedia.org/w/index.php?title=Analysis&oldid=917857646

Anthropocene. (n.d.). In *Wikipedia*. Retrieved October 25, 2019, from https://en.wikipedia.org/w/index.php?title=Anthropocene&oldid=922635524

Assmann, A. (2009, May 18). Individuelles Bildgedächtnis und kollektive Erinnerung. Retrieved from https://www.boell.de/de/demokratie/kulturaustausch-6769.html

Bézier curve. (n.d.). In *Wikipedia*. Retrieved October 26, 2019, from https://en.wikipedia.org/w/index.php?title=B%C3%A9zier_curve&oldid=920964785

Bill, M. (2008). *Funktion und Funktionalismus: Schriften 1945–1988.* Bern: Benteli.

Biyani, G. (2013, May 5). Explained: The actual difference between growth hacking and marketing. Retrieved from https://thenextweb.com/insider/2013/05/05/the-actual-difference-between-growth-hacking-and-marketing-explained/

Boeree, C. G. (1991, August 21). Causes and reasons: The mechanics of anticipation. Retrieved from https://webspace.ship.edu/cgboer/anticipation.html

Bott, H., Grassl, G., & Anders, S. (Eds.). (2013). *Nachhaltige Stadtplanung: Konzepte für nachhaltige Quartiere.* Munich: Detail.

Christensson, P. (2006). Metadata. Retrieved from https://techterms.com/definition/metadata

Clark, I., Sutherland, J., & Young, G. (1995). Keynote speech presented at Cultural mapping symposium and workshop, Australia.

Cloud computing. (n.d.). In *Wikipedia*. Retrieved October 26, 2019, from https://en.wikipedia.org/w/index.php?title=Cloud_computing&oldid=922510176

Cognitive Space. (n.d.). Retrieved November 9, 2019, from http://hybridspacelab.net/project/cognitive-space/

Communication (n.d.). In *Wikipedia.* Retrieved October 26, 2019, from https://en.wikipedia.org/w/index.php?title=Communication&oldid=922969619

Cooper, A., Reimann, R., & Cronin, D. (2007). *About Face 3: The essentials of interaction design.* Indianapolis, IN: Wiley.

Creative Commons. (2019, October 1). Frequently asked questions. Retrieved from https://creativecommons.org/faq/#what-is-creative-commons-and-what-do-you-do

Cultural code. (n.d.). In *Oxford Reference.* Retrieved October 26, 2019, from http://www.oxfordreference.com/view/10.1093/oi/authority.20110803095652803

Cultural mapping. (2017, July 4). Retrieved from https://bangkok.unesco.org/content/cultural-mapping

Daheim, C., & Wintermann, O. (2016). *2050: Die Zukunft der Arbeit; Ergebnisse einer internationalen Delphi-Studie des Millennium Project.* Bertelsmann Stiftung. Retrieved from https://www.bertelsmann-stiftung.de/fileadmin/files/BSt/Publikationen/GrauePublikationen/BST_Delphi_Studie_2016.pdf

Database. (n.d.). In *Wikipedia.* Retrieved October 27, 2019, from https://en.wikipedia.org/w/index.php?title=Database&oldid=917129682

Default (computer science). (n.d.). In *Wikipedia.* Retrieved October 29, 2019, from https://en.wikipedia.org/w/index.php?title=Default_(computer_science)&oldid=916335504

Digital Literacy. (n.d.). In *Wikipedia.* Retrieved October 28, 2019, from https://en.wikipedia.org/w/index.php?title=Digital_literacy&oldid=922708780

DIN Standards Committee Ergonomics. (2011). Ergonomics of human-system interaction – Part 210: Human-centred design for interactive systems (ISO 9241-210:2010). Retrieved from https://www.din.de/en/getting-involved/standards-committees/naerg/standards/wdc-beuth:din21:135399380?destinationLanguage=&sourceLanguage=

Doorey, M. (2019, January 23). James J. Gibson. In *Encyclopaedia Britannica.* Retrieved October 25, 2019, from https://www.britannica.com/biography/James-J-Gibson#ref1174842

Dunne, A., & Raby, F. (2007). Critical design FAQ. Retrieved from http://dunneandraby.co.uk/content/bydandr/13/0

Empirical research. (n.d.). In *Wikipedia.* Retrieved October 27, 2019, from https://en.wikipedia.org/w/index.php?title=Empirical_research&oldid=915854140

Entrepreneurship. (n.d.). In *BusinessDictionary.com.* Retrieved October 27, 2019, from http://www.businessdictionary.com/definition/entrepreneurship.html

EPEA. (2016, December 29). Cradle to Cradle®: Innovation, quality and good design. Retrieved from https://epea-hamburg.com/cradle-to-cradle/

Fraunhofer. (n.d.). Meteoric growth: The Internet of Things is scaling exponentially. Retrieved October 28, 2019, from https://www.internet-der-dinge.de/en.html

Gamp, J., & Gschwend, L. (2017, July 30). Der Wahrheit verpflichtet. *Süddeutsche Zeitung.* Retrieved from http://www.sueddeutsche.de/wirtschaft/forum-der-wahrheit-verpflichtet-1.3609138

German Advisory Council on Global Change (WBGU). (2019). Towards our common digital future: Summary. Berlin: WBGU

Goodwin, C., & Duranti, A. (1992). Rethinking context: An introduction. In C. Goodwin & A. Duranti (Eds.), *Rethinking context: Language as an interactive phenomenon* (pp. 1–42). Cambridge: Cambridge University Press.

Haff, P. (2014, August). Humans and technology in the Anthropocene: Six rules. *The Anthropocene Review,* 1(2), 126–136.

Haptic perception. (n.d.). In *Wikipedia.* Retrieved October 29, 2019, from https://en.wikipedia.org/w/index.php?title=Haptic_perception&oldid=911662963

Heuristic. (n.d.). In *Wikipedia.* Retrieved October 27, 2019, from https://en.wikipedia.org/w/index.php?title=Heuristic&oldid=922589039

Hintikka, J. J. (2019). Philosophy of logic. In *Encyclopaedia Britannica.* Retrieved October 25, 2019, https://www.britannica.com/topic/philosophy-of-logic

Human-centered design. (n. d.). In *Wikipedia*. Retrieved October 28, 2019, from https://en.wikipedia.org/w/index.php?title=Human-centered_design&oldid=919716471

Intellectual Property. (2017, December 1). Retrieved from https://ec.europa.eu/growth/industry/intellectual-property_en

Interactivity. (n. d.). In *Wikipedia*. Retrieved November 10, 2019, from https://en.wikipedia.org/w/index.php?title=Interactivity&oldid=920153305

Interfacedesign. (n. d.). Retrieved October 28, 2019, from https://www.fh-potsdam.de/studieren/fachbereiche/design/studiengaenge/interfacedesign/

Intermediate good. (n. d.). In *Wikipedia*. Retrieved October 28, 2019, from https://en.wikipedia.org/w/index.php?title=Intermediate_good&oldid=901737151

Iteration. (n. d.). In *Wikipedia*. Retrieved October 28, 2019, from https://en.wikipedia.org/w/index.php?title=Iteration&oldid=922617261

Jonas, W. (2012). Exploring the swampy ground. In W. Jonas & S. Grand (Eds.), *Mapping design research* (pp. 11–42). Basel: Birkhäuser.

Klein, G. (2007, Feb 8). Anticipation: How do we prepare ourselves for the unexpected? Retrieved from https://www.psychologytoday.com/us/blog/seeing-what-others-dont/201702/anticipation

Laboratory. (n. d.). In *Wikipedia*. Retrieved October 28, 2019, from https://en.wikipedia.org/w/index.php?title=Laboratory&oldid=922018025

Lemelson-MIT Program. (2003). *The architecture of invention*. Cambridge, MA: School of Engineering, Massachusetts Institute of Technology.

Maldei, T., Koole, S. L., & Baumann, N. (2019, October). Listening to your intuition in the face of distraction: Effects of taxing working memory on accuracy and bias of intuitive judgments of semantic coherence. *Cognition 191*.

Medeiros, J. (2017, December). Stephen Hawking: "I fear AI may replace humans altogether". *Wired*. Retrieved from http://www.wired.co.uk/article/stephen-hawking-interview-alien-life-climate-change-donald-trump

Merholz, P., & Skinner, K. (2016). *Org design for design orgs: Building and managing in-house design teams*. Sebastopol, CA: O'Reilly Media.

Mieg, H. A. (2010). Focused cognition: Information integration and complex problem solving by top inventors. In K. L. Mosier & U. M. Fischer (Eds.), *Informed by knowledge: Expert performance in complex situations* (pp. 41–54). London: Taylor & Francis.

Mockup. (n. d.). In *Wikipedia*. Retrieved October 28, 2019, from https://en.wikipedia.org/w/index.php?title=Mockup&oldid=898057721

Modell. (n. d.). In *Wikipedia*. Retrieved October 28, 2019, from https://en.wikipedia.org/w/index.php?title=Modell&oldid=192500296

Müller, B. (2017, January 6). Intuition is the key to good design. *Modus*. Retrieved from https://modus.medium.com/in-defence-of-intuition-f924ab82f76b#.jgvxl120t

Näger, S. (2007). *Literacy: Kinder entdecken Buch-, Erzähl- und Schriftkultur*. Freiburg: Herder.

Noë, A. (2006). *Action in perception*. Cambridge, MA: MIT Press.

Noë, A. (2013, January 30). Why is consciousness so baffling? [Video file]. Retrieved from https://www.youtube.com/watch?v=1aPeWc7Um1A&t=399s

Norman, D. (2016). Don Norman: The term UX [Video file]. Retrieved from https://www.youtube.com/watch?v=9BdtGjoIN4E

Obsolescence. (n. d.). In *Wikipedia*. Retrieved October 29, 2019, from https://en.wikipedia.org/w/index.php?title=Obsolescence&oldid=917565924

Oxford University Press (OUP). (2019a). Art. Retrieved from https://www.lexico.com/en/definition/art

Oxford University Press (OUP). (2019b). Combination. Retrieved from https://www.lexico.com/en/definition/combination

Oxford University Press (OUP). (2019c). Method. Retrieved from https://www.lexico.com/en/definition/method

Oxford University Press (OUP). (2019d). Synthesis. Retrieved from https://www.lexico.com/en/definition/synthesis

Oxford University Press (OUP). (2019e). Visual. Retrieved from https://www.lexico.com/en/definition/visual

Parameter. (2018). In *Artopium: Online Music Dictionary*. Retrieved October 29, 2019, from https://musicterms.artopium.com/p/Parameter.htm

Pfeffer, F. (2014). *To do: Die neue Rolle der Gestaltung in einer veränderten Welt*. Mainz: Herman Schmidt.

Pictogram. (n. d.). In *Wikipedia*. Retrieved October 29, 2019, from https://en.wikipedia.org/w/index.php?title=Pictogram&oldid=921165475

Poli, R. (2009). The many aspects of anticipation. *Foresight: The journal of future studies, strategic thinking and policy, 12*(3), 7–17, http://dx.doi.org/10.1108/14636681011049839

Preset. (n. d.). In *Wikipedia*. Retrieved October 29, 2019, from https://en.wikipedia.org/w/index.php?title=Preset&oldid=888776411

Process. (n. d.). In *BusinessDictionary.com*. Retrieved November 10, 2019, from https://en.wikipedia.org/w/index.php?title=Process&oldid=921215668

Public value. (n. d.). In *Wikipedia*. Retrieved October 29, 2019, from http://www.businessdictionary.com/definition/process.html

Research. (n. d.). In *Oxford Reference*. Retrieved October 30, 2019, from https://www.lexico.com/en/definition/research

Romero-Tejedor, F., & Van den Boom, H. (2013). *Die semiotische Haut der Dinge: Felicidad Romero-Tejedor im Gespräch mit Holger van den Boom*. Kassel: Kassel University Press.

Schmidt, O. (2012). *Hybride Räume: Filmwelten im Hollywood-Kino der Jahrtausendwende*. Marburg: Schüren Verlag.

Schön, D. A. (1983). *The reflective practitioner: How professionals think in action*. New York Basic Books.

Searle, J. (1980). Minds, brains, and programs. *Behavioral and Brain Sciences, 3*(3), 417–457.

Semiotics. (n. d.). In *Wikipedia*. Retrieved October 30, 2019, from https://en.wikipedia.org/w/index.php?title=Semiotics&oldid=920235285

Service design. (n. d.). In *Wikipedia*. Retrieved October 30, 2019, from https://en.wikipedia.org/w/index.php?title=Service_design&oldid=917921991

Sheppard, B., Sarrazin, H., Kouyoumjian, G., & Dore, F. (2018, October). The business value of design. *McKinsey Quarterly*. Retrieved from https://www.mckinsey.com/business-functions/mckinsey-design/our-insights/the-business-value-of-design

Social interaction. (n. d.). In *Psychology Wiki*. Retrieved November 10, 2019, from https://psychology.wikia.org/wiki/Social_interaction

Strategy. (n. d.). In *BusinessDictionary.com*. Retrieved October 30, 2019, from http://www.businessdictionary.com/definition/strategy.html

System. (n. d.). In *Wikipedia*. Retrieved October 31, 2019, from https://en.wikipedia.org/w/index.php?title=System&oldid=923670695

The concept of model: Definitions and types. (n. d.). Retrieved October 28, 2019, from http://www.muellerscience.com/ENGLISH/Theconceptofmodel.definitions.htm

The Editors of Encyclopaedia Britannica. (2012). Intuition. In *Encyclopaedia Britannica*. Retrieved October 28, 2019, from https://www.britannica.com/topic/intuition

Tubik Studio. (2018, May 8). UX design glossary: How to use affordances in user interfaces. Retrieved from https://uxplanet.org/ux-design-glossary-how-to-use-affordances-in-user-interfaces-393c8e9686e4

Van der Waerden, B. L., & Taisback, C. M. (2019, August 2). Euclid. In *Encyclopaedia Britannica*. Retrieved October 25, 2019, from https://www.britannica.com/biography/Euclid-Greek-mathematician

Virtual reality. (n. d.). In *Wikipedia*. Retrieved October 31, 2019, from https://en.wikipedia.org/w/index.php?title=Virtual_reality&oldid=922835734

Virtuality (disambiguation). (n. d.). In *Wikipedia*. Retrieved November 10, 2019, from https://en.wikipedia.org/w/index.php?title=Virtuality_(disambiguation)&oldid=918396086

Virtuality (philosophy). (n. d.). In *Wikipedia*. Retrieved October 31, 2019, from https://en.wikipedia.org/w/index.php?title=Virtuality_(philosophy)&oldid=897002306

Vogt, M. (2013). The great transformation: How the shift in values is generating policy shift. Retrieved from https://www.goethe.de/en/kul/ges/20368938.html

Weber, E. H. (1851). *Die Lehre vom Tastsinne und Gemeingefühle auf Versuche gegründet*. Braunschweig: Friedrich Vieweg.

WIPO (World Intellectual Property Organization). (n. d.). What is intellectual property? Retrieved November 10, 2019, from https://www.wipo.int/about-ip/en/

Wizard of Oz experiment. (n. d.). In *Wikipedia*. Retrieved October 31, 2019, from https://en.wikipedia.org/w/index.php?title=Wizard_of_Oz_experiment&oldid=916055662

Photo credits

17: shutterstock/Faina Gurevich **25:** Julia Bohle, Arina Iurikin, Nina Merkusheva, Maike Panz, Tabea Rocke, Lydia Wilke
28–73: project: Julia Bohle, Tabea Rocke, Lydia Wilke; photos: Julia Bohle, Tabea Rocke, Lydia Wilke and Alexandra Martini (AM)
108: top: Meera Lehr, bottom: Bianca Streich **109:** Paul Anker **110:** left: Jasmin Kappler, right: Alvaro Garcia **111:** Enzo
Leclerq **112:** Rahel Armbröster, Julia Deege, Alicia Ruge, Anna-Maria Zinn; bottom: Mario Homburg, Moira Berit Joachim,
Dominik Manikowski, Jose Ernesto Rodriguez, Nina Tschirner **113:** Mona Salimi **114:** project: Theresa Hauff, Lena Hegger,
Natascha Lawiszus; photo left: AM **115:** top: Caspar Kirsch; bottom left: NN, right: Ina Hengstler, photos: Roberta
Bergmann **116:** project: Samira Akhavan; photo: AM **117:** project: Fabian Archner, Johanna Olm, Felix Zeitz, photo: AM
118: Edmundo Mejía Galindo, Felix Landwehr, Johannah Langsdorf, Soo Min Kwon **119:** Nadezda Kuzmina **120:** Diana
Belodedov, Clara Schwerin, Oriana Striebeck **121:** Theresa Bastek, Caterina Plenzick, Jan Simon Veicht **122/123:** project:
Paul Anker, Fanny Belling, Melissa Kramer, Pavel Shergin; photo: AM **124:** Martina Del Ben, Julius Lehniger, Paulina Rynowiecka,
Nicolai Thoma **125:** Fabian Lange, Jannis Riethmüller **126:** project: Anna Heib, photo: AM **127:** project: Nina Komarova-
Zelinskaya, Paul Roeder, Miriam Zanzinger, Jonas Wolff; photo: AM **128/129:** screenshots: Gal Yaron Mayersohn; supervision:
Professor Anne Quirynen and Professor Alexandra Martini **132:** Martina Del Ben, Julius Lehniger, Paulina Rynowiecka, Nicolai
Thoma **133:** Omar Abdel-moaty, Zlatko Dulic, Ronja Schratzenstaller **134/135:** Carmen Voigt **136/137:** Daniel
Birnbaum **138/139:** Andrea Biedermann, Clara von Schwerin, Felix Thiel, Philip Wiemer **139/141/142:** Friedemann Gutsche,
Stephane Flesch, Marcus Maybauer, Thomas Miebach **143:** AM **144:** Pia Marktl **145:** project: Maren Hinze, Selina Heursen,
Clara Keseberg; photo: AM **146/147:** Andrea Biedermann, George Croissant, Maike Panz, Stefan Rumjanzew **148/149:**
Mandy Puchert, Celia Marchena, Carmen Voigt **152:** Andrea Biedermann, Clara von Schwerin, Felix Thiel, Philip Wiemer
153: Mehran Djojan, Florian Dymke, Johannah Langsdorf, Miriam Zanzinger **154:** Caroline Ammer, Felix Landwehr, Jacqueline
Röttger, Marlies Wieking **155:** Mehran Djojan, Florian Dymke, Johannah Langsdorf, Miriam Zanzinger **156/157:** Mario
Homburg, Moira Berit Joachim, Dominik Manikowski, Jose Ernesto Rodriguez, Nina Tschirner **158/159:** Magdalena Dziewit,
Arthur Mr. Fauske, Bela Lehrnickel, Dennis Ruf **160:** Nele Zielke **161:** Arina Iurikin, Johanna Mellenthin, Felix Müller, Isabel
Redecke **162/163:** Pelle Dwertmann, Hanno Fennel, Philip Wiemer **164:** Adrian Manke, Maria Pantke, Maike Panz
165: Joseph Ribbe, Lorenz Seidlein, Lena Weidinger, Lukas Wiegand **166/167:** Johannes Heinrich, Katrin Junghans, Gabriella
Lanyi, Celia Staffa **168/169:** Moritz Freudenberg, Tilo Krüger, Danai Moshona, Oriana Striebeck **170/171:** Julian Krischker,
Robin Marx, Philipp Pusch, Magdalena Zagorski **174:** Marlies Wieking **175:** Edmundo Mejía Galindo, Felix Landwehr, Johannah
Langsdorf, Soo Min Kwon **176/177:** photos: Johanna Penitzka, Lorenz von Seidlein, Till Milan Troll, photo left: Adrian Manke,
Maria Pantke, Maike Panz **178:** Josephin Kunze **179:** bottom: Maria Pantke, top: Mandy Puchert **180:** Julian Braun, Isabel
Latza **181:** photo: Caterina Plenzick **182/183:** Ruslan Putc, © by Adobe Inc 2017, Adobe® Photoshop® / www.adobe.com/
de **184/185:** Ann Bahrs, Karoline Große, Brenda Jorde, Gesche Amalie Ringer **186:** Sofie Karlotta Maurer **187:** Julia
Bohle **188:** Anja Lutz, Thuy Tien Vo, Vincenzo Werner **189:** Willi von Essen, Moritz Gnann, Sahra Lietzkow, Viccha Kren
192: Felix Thiel **193:** bottom: Charlotte Gruchot, Heike Otten, Daniela Pusch, Marc Philip Sommer; top: Felix Landwehr
194: left: Foto AM; right Daniel Boubet **195:** top: Jan Veicht: bottom: Verena Haltenberger, Theresa Hannig, Carla Schewe,
Carlotta Thomas, Nushin Yazdani **196:** Samira Akavan, Lisa-Marie Brüning, Justyna Ligocka, Svenja Teitge, Felix Thiel
198: Caterina Plenzick **199:** project: Edmundo Mejía Galindo, Felix Landwehr, Johannah Langsdorf, Soo Min Kwon, photos:
AM **200:** Sarah Horvath, Paula Schuster, Phillipp Steinacher, Nadia Zeissig **201:** Miriam Becker, Lea Bräuer, Fabian Lange,
Lola Mariella Ritter, Anna-Lena Wolfrum **202/203:** Adrian Manke, Maria Pantke, Maike Panz **204/205:** Charlotte Gruchot,
Heike Otten, Daniela Pusch, Marc Philip Sommer **206/207:** project: Jannis Specks, Luisa Preiss, Marc Philip Sommer, photo
right: Jannis Specks **208/209:** project: Melissa Kramer; supervision: Roman Grasy and Professor Alexandra Martini, photos:
AM and Melissa Kramer **212:** Caroline Ammer **213:** Marlies Wieking **214:** top: Jakob Werner; bottom: Lena Schröder
215: Arina Iurikin **216:** Jasmin Hannig **217:** Lena Wallacher **218:** project top: Diana Beushausen, project bottom: Wolfgang
Albrecht, Marta Carlesso, Leon Jiang, Felix Köpke; photos: AM **219:** Amelie Lichtenberg, Lola Marella Ritter
220/221: Daniel Birnbaum, Daniela Pusch, Paula Schuster, Marc Philip Sommer **222:** Jannis Hektor, Syuga Raytila, Peter
Schwarz, Max Tamm **223:** Lars Höft **224:** Arina Iurikin, Nina Merkushava **225:** project: Aaron Schwerdtfeger, Peter Schwarz,
Robin Wenzel; supervision: Professor Myriel Milicevic and Professor Alexandra Martini, photo: AM **226:** Caroline Ammer
227: Ivo Erichsen, Dennis Ruf, Elias Suske, Claire Vogt **237:** Hoffotografen Berlin

The Author

Thanks

Alexandra Martini is a designer and professor for design at the University of Applied Sciences Potsdam, Germany. She teaches interdisciplinary space, materiality, perception, and methodology. She supervises cooperation projects, conducting research on sustainable urban development and the experimental creative process.

Martini studied design at the University of the Arts (UdK) Berlin, the Escuela Superior del Diseño Elisava, Barcelona and the Royal College of Art in London, Department School of Architecture. After teaching temporary architecture at the Escuela Superior de Diseño y Interiores (ESDI) Barcelona, she was professor of design at the University of Fine Arts (HBK) Braunschweig. She established a reputation with her Berlin office for design MARTINI, MEYER. In parallel to this, she led workshops on the creative process at the Association of Arts and Culture of the German Economy at the Federation of German Industries. In terms of design policy, Martini has been active for the Berlin Senate, the Goethe-Institut, and UNESCO.

www.alexandramartini.com

I am particularly grateful to all those who were involved in this project from the beginning and contributed their interest and commitment:
Nadja Fischer, Arwed Messmer, Professor Wolfgang Jonas, Professor Harald Mieg, Maike Panz, and Annett Zahn.
Special thanks goes to my family, Laura, Antonia, Bernd, Ursula, and Karl Martini.

I would also like to thank the following for their support and advice:
Simon Cowper, Carsten Eisfeld, Katja Frick, Marie Güsewell, Dr. Ulrike Hasemann, Dr. Katrin von Kap-herr, Stefanie Klein, Jörg Misch, Katrin Neubert, Professor Boris Müller, Maria Pantke, Christin Renner, Zulima Saenz, and Donatus Wolf.

I am grateful too for the productive relationship with my cooperation partners:
Professor Myriel Milicevic, Professor Anne Quirynen, Professor Karl-Heinz Winkens, Frieder Söling (Berlin Waste Management/BSR), Matthias Einhoff and Philip Horst (Center for Art and Urbanistics, ZK/U Berlin), Eckwerk (Holzmarkt e.G.), and Potsdam Institute for Climate Impact Research (PIK).

A big thanks goes to all students and alumni of the Potsdam University of Applied Sciences and the University of Art (HBK) Braunschweig, whose works contribute to this book.

Colophon

Copyediting and Translation: Simon Cowper
Graphic Design: Carsten Eisfeld
Typeface: Neue Haas Grotesk
Reproductions: Arwed Messmer

BIS Publishers
Building Het Sieraad
Postjesweg 1
1057 DT Amsterdam
The Netherlands
T +31 (0)20 515 02 30
bis@bispublishers.com
www.bispublishers.com

ISBN 978-90-6369-573-6

our methods turn out to be ideal. Go ahead.